REALLY OLD, LIKE FORTY FIVE

Tamsin Oglesby

REALLY OLD, LIKE FORTY FIVE

OBERON BOOKS
LONDON

Published in 2010 by Oberon Books Ltd
521 Caledonian Road, London N7 9RH
Tel: 020 7607 3637 / Fax: 020 7607 3629
e-mail: info@oberonbooks.com
www.oberonbooks.com

Really Old, Like Forty Five © Tamsin Oglesby 2010

A catalogue record for this book is available from the British Library.

ISBN: 978-1-84002-982-6

Cover photo by Ralph Crane (Getty Images)
Cover design by Charlotte Wilkinson

Printed in Great Britain by CPI Antony Rowe, Chippenham

Really Old, Like Forty Five was first performed at the National Theatre's Cottesloe Theatre, London on 27 January 2010, with the following cast:

MILLIE Lucy May Barker
MIKE Paul Bazely
CATHY Amelia Bullmore
AMANDA Tanya Franks
ROBBIE Gawn Grainger
DYLAN Thomas Jordan
MIMI Michela Meazza
LYN Judy Parfitt
MONROE Paul Ritter
ALICE Marcia Warren

Director Anna Mackmin
Designer Lez Brotherston
Lighting Designer Mark Henderson
*Video Designer*s Mark Grimmer with Lysander Ashton
Choreographer Scarlett Mackmin
Sound Designer Christopher Shutt

Characters

LYN
Sister of Alice and Robbie (middle sibling)

ALICE
Sister of Lyn and Robbie (youngest sibling)

ROBBIE
Brother of Lyn and Alice (oldest sibling)

CATHY
Lyn's daughter

MILLIE
16, Lyn's adopted granddaughter

DYLAN
13, Alice's grandson

MONROE
Government policy official

AMANDA
Researcher

MIKE
Accountant

MIMI
Robot Nurse, played by a dancer

Act One

SCENE ONE

BAR AT THE THEATRE.

> *CATHY, ALICE, LYN and DYLAN assemble around a table. ALICE settles and gets out her knitting.*

CATHY: Are we enjoying the play then?

ALICE: Oh it's marvellous darling, absolutely splendid production.

LYN: I hate Shakespeare.

CATHY: You chose it.

LYN: I keep forgetting. Anyway there wasn't anything else.

ALICE: What about that thing with the man from you know where the police are hypnotists and the criminals all end up naked?

LYN: You mean the comedian?

ALICE: No no the other one. The funny actor with the moustache.

LYN: Oh he's dead.

ALICE: No he's not. He's in the West End.

LYN: No, he *died*.

ALICE: He's not. He didn't

LYN: He did. It was all over the front page.

ALICE: Oh *died*. You mean you mean they didn't laugh?

LYN: Why would they laugh?

ALICE: He's a comedian.

LYN: I'm not talking about the comedian. I'm talking about the other one. With the moustache. He's dead.

ALICE: Really?

LYN: Yes, remember. Fell out of a hospital window. Drugs or something.

ALICE: Funny place to do drugs. Well I suppose he was a comedian.

LYN: No no no NO that's what I'm saying, oh god. What *is* the boy doing?

CATHY: I don't know. Alice?

ALICE: What're you doing, darling?

DYLAN: Trying to get all the lemonade into the glass without lifting the bottle.

LYN: Why?

ALICE: Just be careful.

LYN: You'll spill it.

DYLAN: No I won't.

LYN: He'll spill it.

ALICE: I'm sure he won't.

DYLAN: I won't. Look.

LYN: I really don't think this is a suitable place in which to conduct experiments on surface tension.

ALICE: If you hold it a bit more – there, that's it.

LYN: Did we ask Robbie to get some of those you know, those, you know

CATHY: What?

LYN: You know, with the eyes. Nuts. Shaped like eyes, you know, those little eye-shaped ones that taste a bit like like like almonds.

CATHY: Almonds.

LYN: Almonds, yes, yes, yes, of course, almonds!

CATHY: Almonds taste like almonds.

Beat.

LYN: Oh I do wish you'd stop *knitting*.

ALICE: Why?

LYN: Are you trying to make a point?

ALICE: No. I'm trying to make a rumper suit.

LYN: How are Joseph Barnaby and co?

ALICE: I wish you wouldn't say it like that.

LYN: Another bouncing baby Barnaby is it?

ALICE: He seems quite healthy, yes.

LYN: Another boisterous bullish Barnaby boy for you?

ALICE: You're talking about Dylan's father, Lyn.

LYN: More of his pugnacious progeny peopling the planet

ALICE: He's only got three. It's hardly

LYN: Adding to the clan. Waving the family flag and stocking up the ancestral heritage. Jumping about in the ha ha

ALICE: Lyn, stop it.

LYN: I do think it's very rum they couldn't find you a cupboard or something to sleep in. Size of that pile. You'd think there'd be a box room for a small granny under the stairs wouldn't you.

ALICE: It's not like that. I told you. She works and he's never there.

LYN: Well then you'd have the run of it wouldn't you? Perfect.

ALICE: You want me to move out?

LYN: I won't be around for ever you know. And you wouldn't want to trip over your dressing gown and crack your head open only to be discovered two months later because of the smell in the drains.

ALICE: Anyway I've seen you knitting. You could get your own grandchild.

LYN: You cannot knit a grandchild.

ALICE: I'm talking about the adoption thing.

LYN: I do not want to adopt a bastard.

ALICE: They're not bastards.

LYN: They don't have parents.

CATHY: That would make them orphans.

ALICE: They do have parents. It's just their parents can't look after them.

LYN: Well if their parents can't look after them I certainly can't.

ALICE: Because they're working, or estranged, or whatever.

LYN: I don't want to talk about this. I'm going round the world and I'm stopping off in Australia to see my cousin.

CATHY: Mum, look. We've had this conversation. You know my flat is too small. And you're allowed to stay in your house if you're sharing.

LYN: What conversation? That's not the conversation I'm having.

Pause.

CATHY: Oh where is your brother? We should go.

ALICE: Why? Is it the curfew?

CATHY: No it's not the curfew. It's the end of the interval.

LYN: Do we have to?

CATHY: What?

LYN: Do we have to go back in there?

CATHY: What do you mean?

LYN: All that *acting*. I can't bear it. Can't we just…go?

CATHY: What, walk out?

LYN: What do you think Alice?

ALICE: I don't mind really.

CATHY: *(Softly.)* Jesus.

DYLAN: I don't want to leave. It hasn't finished yet.

> *ROBBIE appears. He looks as though he's in his sixties but is dressed younger.*

ALICE: Oh hoorah. drinks.

ROBBIE: Do I look like an *old man*?

LYN: Yes.

ALICE: No, dear, of course you don't.

ROBBIE: Do I?

CATHY: Why?

ROBBIE: Do I look like an old man for fuck's sake do I?

CATHY: No, why, what's the matter?

ROBBIE: I've been standing at the bar for half an hour, this arsehole behind me, bald corporate fucker in a sharp suit what's he doing here anyway in his fucking suit don't suppose he even knows what he's watching but he knew I was before him because he was standing right behind me, I'm just about to order and he butts in, I can't believe, shouted right over my head because he's tall, I said excuse me *mate,* excuse me – I was polite but firm – excuse me but you know perfectly well I was before you and he said Jesus Christ he said calm down *old man.* I was calm. I fucking was calm before he said that. He's the one with no hair. He's the bald bastard. I've got more hair on my head than he has on his whole body. Fuck's sake.

DYLAN: Uncle Robbie swore.

ROBBIE: Bald fucking prick.

DYLAN: You shouldn't swear Uncle Robbie.

CATHY: Dylan not now.

ALICE: No drinks then.

DYLAN: You should of just got out your blade and shanked him.

LYN: So what happened?

ROBBIE: You want to know what happened?

CATHY: Yes, what happened?

DYLAN: Blow his head off *(Shooting noises.)*

ROBBIE: I'll tell you what happened.

DYLAN: What happened Uncle Robbie?

Beat.

ROBBIE: I hit him.

CATHY: You what?

DYLAN: Oh Sick.

LYN: Oh dear.

DYLAN: Where?

ROBBIE: On the head.

CATHY: You – how – oh god.

ROBBIE: Not hard. Just, you know

DYLAN: Was there blood?

ROBBIE: Sort of head butt sort of thing

ALICE: What did he say?

CATHY: You head-butted a man at the bar of the National Theatre ?

DYLAN: Did he, like, bleed everywhere?

ROBBIE: There was a bit of blood, yes.

CATHY: Right, that's it.

ROBBIE: It's alright. He's gone now.

CATHY: Where?

ROBBIE: I don't know. He just left.

DYLAN: He might be dead. Is he dead? Bet you he's dead.

CATHY: Oh shuttup Dylan. My god, Robbie, what's got into you?

DYLAN: Wait till I tell Matt. My Great Uncle battered a city boy. He's gonna be well impressed.

ALICE: Are you alright?

ROBBIE: Do I look alright?

ALICE: You look marvellous darling. Do you want to sit down?

CATHY: Christ.

ROBBIE: I don't need to sit down. I'm fine. Aren't we going back in?

CATHY: They don't want to.

ROBBIE: It wasn't that bad.

LYN: Yes well it's not supposed to be medicine is it? It's supposed to be fun.

CATHY: It's a tragedy.

LYN: You're still supposed to enjoy it. We were having a nice chat. So. If I did adopt one of these bastard orphan children, would I get to choose?

ALICE: What do you mean?

LYN: It would have to be a baby.

ALICE: Everyone wants babies.

CATHY: Well I'm going back in.

DYLAN: Yeah we're going back in.

LYN: Oh why don't you all just sit down and relax, have a nice cup of tea and a piece of cake?

CATHY: You've already had both those things.

ALICE: Have we got time to go to the ladies?

CATHY: No.

LYN: What do you mean? I have not had tea.

CATHY: You have.

LYN: What cake did I have? I don't remember a cake.

CATHY: Lemon poppyseed.

LYN: When? *(She stares at her plate, trying to fathom it.)*

CATHY: Look. Will you all please stop pissing around and just get back in that theatre then we can go home and you can stuff yourself with cake and tea and chocolate all bloody night. *Please.*

Beat.

DYLAN: Aunty Cathy swore. Twice.

CATHY: I said *please.*

SCENE TWO

MONROE addresses a conference from a podium.

The speech is simultaneously broadcast from a screen against a background of diverse footage representing old age and infirmity.

A street scene: the old people are circled and highlighted for the various obstructions they seem to cause with their sticks and buggies and general lack of purpose.

A hospital scene: elderly patients on drips, struggling and sleeping.

These scenes are contrasted with those of:

Grandparents: as they read stories to small children; swing them in the air; play happy families.

MONROE: Anyone walking through the streets of our cities, towns and even villages today has to navigate their way through them. They wander, without purpose or direction, sometimes alone, at other times in gaggles, and very often, it seems, just in the way. What exactly are they doing? We are confronted with our own impatience. Why are they not at home? We all know the feeling. Irritation. Guilt. Disgust. Pity. We're only human. How are we, as individuals, supposed to cope with what is becoming the single most pressing social and economic problem of our times?

The number of people over the age of sixty has reached a staggering thirty eight percent of the population. Now there was a time when these people would be surrounded by their families. This is no longer the case. Women have long been at work among men, and children, together with the old, are increasingly farmed out to institutions or raised in the absence of a proper family carer. There is, quite simply, no-one at home.

The problem is twofold. Not only do we have an excess of old people but the number of under sixteens brought up by single or absent parents has doubled in the last five years.

Let me start with the elderly population. Apart from being numerous, our old people are, on average, older than they've ever been. One in six is living beyond their natural life span and means. Recipients of other people's organs, sustained by the transfusion of other people's blood, kidneys, livers, donated by people from different countries, sometimes even different *species* (I refer to the pensioner with the cow's liver, the octogenarian with the heart of a pig).

So. We have learnt to live longer. All well and good. But have we learnt to live better? We have eradicated nearly all those diseases of the twentieth century. But still we are haunted, eluded, by those of a neurodegenerative nature, and let us remind ourselves, lest we should forget, *because they certainly will,* that ten percent of the population now suffer from Alzheimer's. It is a universal and unprecedented situation which, having reached epidemic proportions, can no longer be borne by the individual. Or ignored.

So, the under sixteens and the over sixties. What we are proposing is a programme which attempts to diffuse both these demographic timebombs.

I have been advised by leading American epidemiologist, Dr. Larry Morton, that, when overpopulation occurs within the animal kingdom they have learnt to develop strategies for the purpose of self regulation. Chimpanzees, for example, devour each other. I'm not suggesting, obviously, that we eat our old people. Apart from the ethical question, people are, as I understand it, of dubious nutritional value once past the age of child rearing. No. What I am proposing is a working economical system which regulates the imbalance in our society, which supports the elderly and cares for its young. The benefit of our scheme is that it will return the streets to some semblance of order. It will restore the notion of proper family life in our society. It will occupy and involve a large swathe of otherwise inactive members of society. And it will generate income and consequently save the average householder approximately seventy pounds a year in Health costs.

My good friend, Larry Morton assures us that we have gone as far as we can down the road of animal experimentation in relation to medical cures. Even if the hamster could remember how many times he's gone round the wheel he couldn't possibly tell us. So. And. What we now need, on a large scale, is people. To which end I am proud to announce the opening of our flagship hospital, the Ark, which will be playing host to a systematic programme of 'in man' studies. This programme will be in place for all those over the age of retirement, although those already deceased – sorry *diseased* – will have preferential status. And participation in these Trials will be rewarded with long term care of the highest order. There is already every indication that demand for places will be high.

But for the elderly and fit who choose not to do the Trials there are alternatives. It will be the responsibility, no, *privilege,* of these people to take up an active grandparenting role in the community. The BPA has long held that the State is insufficient to the task of child-rearing. Not only is there no better substitute for childcare than the individual – especially among the very young – but the financial burden on the state is in excess of its means. And for those who do neither, who become ill and choose not to take part in medical Trials, there will be, on request, highly qualified staff equipped to assist in the increasingly popular option of Home Deaths.

This is our aim. To return to the elderly a sense of purpose. For without purpose there can be no dignity and without dignity we are barely human. Old age needn't mean redundancy. We have for too long perpetuated the illusion that to live long is in itself a virtue. For as a species we have learnt much and forgotten much. We have discovered how to live longer, but not better. We have learnt to travel, but not to see. And we have not learnt how to die. To let go of life as you let go of a child when it can walk, to say goodbye when you've said everything you want to say, to die when you've given all you have to give. This is our task. To banish forever the association of old age with irrelevance. To give everyone a function, regardless of their age, and to make their last days on earth as fulfilling as they can possibly be.

Applause. Cries of approval from the floor.

SCENE THREE

THE NATURAL HISTORY MUSEUM.

A tank, with a large turtle inside.

LYN, ALICE and MILLIE, watching it.

ALICE: Do you like animals?

MILLIE: Some of them.

ALICE: We thought you'd be too old for the zoo. They said a museum's better.

LYN: How old are you, Millie?

ALICE: Fifteen. She said.

MILLIE: How old are you?

LYN: Oh. Do I have to answer that?

ALICE: You don't have to do anything, Lyn. Just relax.

LYN: My sister's very good with children. She's got hundreds of grandchildren. I've been practising on my nephew, Dylan. He's thirteen.

ALICE: Do you like the turtle?

MILLIE: It's okay.

ALICE: Have you ever seen one like it?

LYN: Of course she hasn't. No-one has. It's without precedent.

MILLIE: It's big.

LYN: Four foot long, but they can grow up to six.

MILLIE: For what it does though, they didn't have to have a live one.

LYN: What do you mean?

MILLIE: They should of got a replicant.

LYN: No, the point is, it's *real*.

MILLIE: Is it though?

LYN: It's *yes* of course it is. It's two hundred and fifty years old. He was probably born, no, he was born before Queen Victoria was even conceived. He's come all the way from the Galapagos islands. He will have met *Charles Darwin*.

MILLIE: Yeah but it doesn't *do* much.

LYN: Well I don't suppose you do much.

ALICE: Lyn.

MILLIE: And it really stinks.

LYN: So, what, would you'd prefer one of those those what'stheword they have that light up and move about on remote control and tell you what it feels like to be an old turtle?

MILLIE: That would be cool.

ALICE: I can tell you what it feels like to be an old turtle.

MILLIE: You shouldn't take creatures out of their natural habitat and transplant them. It's not environmental.

ALICE: If you don't like it we could go and see the stuffed cats.

MILLIE: Nah. They shouldn't of turned his rock. He dies, there'll be blood on their hands.

LYN: He will die. One day soon, he will die.

ALICE: Because he's a living thing.

LYN: Yes because he's a living thing and because he's two hundred and fifty fucking years old. And then that'll be it. Everything he's seen, heard, felt, eaten. Gone.

MILLIE: Well yeah that's sad and everything but it's not like anyone's gonna miss him. Friends and relatives and that.

ALICE: Until the next life. When he might become a deer if he's been good. Or a rabbit. Something you can stroke.

LYN: He's *unique.*

MILLIE: We all are.

Beat.

ALICE: Let's go and see the stuffed cats. They're dead, obviously, but there's a café next door.

MILLIE: No offence but I mean it's not like he knows he's two hundred and fifty years old, is it? It's not like he's aware. He doesn't even – *(She taps the glass.)* see, he's not responding – he doesn't even know we're here.

LYN: Don't do that. Please. You'll frighten him.

MILLIE: It's like those shells you sometimes get in bathrooms, yeah. You go, oh wow, they're so beautiful aren't they amazing and all that but normally – unless they found them theirselves – the people with the shells in the bathrooms – normally they just bought them off someone who bought them off someone who bought them off someone etcetera which isn't such a big deal.

LYN: What are you talking about?

MILLIE: If I found it myself it would be different.

LYN: If you found this turtle yourself it would be different?

MILLIE: It would be amazing. If I was just walking along and I came across a turtle like this

LYN: There is no turtle like this. There are hardly any other turtles like this. That's the point. He's dying out.

MILLIE: Yeah but if there *was.*

LYN: There *isn't.*

ALICE: I had a tortoise when I was little. Used to walk backwards. We called him Stupid. But he wasn't stupid he was quite clever. He'd come when you called his name.

LYN: And where do you imagine finding this turtle? Clapham High Street? In the Thames?

MILLIE: I'm not being funny, I'm just saying. I can't, like, relate to it.

LYN: If it's real. Isn't that enough?

ALICE: It does look very realistic.

LYN: That's because it is real, you twit. *(MILLIE circles the tank again to see better. She taps the glass a few times as she goes.)* I told you it wouldn't work. I did say to them, I was very specific, I said I want a baby, stroke, toddler.

ALICE: Babies are tiring. They match you with someone they think you'll get on with. Just be nicer.

LYN: Look at her.

ALICE: She's lovely.

LYN: We used to struggle with the fourth dimension. They spend so much time in front of two dimensional screens they can barely manage the third.

ALICE: They're not that different to babies really. Teenagers. They still need unconditional love.

LYN: That may be so but they also need to know the difference between what's real and what's rubbish.

ALICE: Obviously, yes, all children need boundaries.

LYN: Boundaries, yes, and goals.

ALICE: They need boundaries and goals and unconditional love.

LYN: I know that.

MILLIE returns. Pause.

MILLIE: Where are these stuffed cats then?

LYN: Go on then, touch it.

MILLIE: What?

LYN: The turtle.

MILLIE: You're not allowed.

ALICE: Lyn

LYN: Touch it, go on. If that's what it takes. Touch it.

ALICE: You're not supposed to cross the line.

MILLIE: There's a piece of tape.

LYN: See what a real turtle feels like. Go on.

ALICE: Stop it, Lyn.

LYN: Alright so let's say, what about if it was in fact a a a a you know, a rabbit? What if they put a rabbit thing inside but didn't tell you they'd put a rabbit inside and pretended it was real?

Beat.

MILLIE: A rabbit?

LYN: Yes you know. One of those automatic..you know …machines… with the motor thing inside

MILLIE: Robot.

LYN: Yes. What if they had put one inside? What if it was one? Should they tell you? Would you feel cheated?

MILLIE: A robot?

LYN: Yes.

Beat.

ALICE: You said *rabbit*. A rabbit inside a turtle.

LYN: Robot.

ALICE: Yes but you said *rabbit*. You said what if they put a rabbit inside a turtle… –

LYN: Yes yes alright. I meant robot.

MILLIE: Is it a robot?

LYN: What if it is?

MILLIE: Do you think? Come on, speedy, come on. Well it's not got voice recognition.

LYN: So it doesn't matter to you? That it's authentic. The only thing that matters to you, the only thing that would move you to *wonder* is if you found it and you could pick it up and you owned it. If it was yours.

MILLIE: I don't know.

ALICE: She's only a child.

MILLIE: I'm not.

LYN: No she's not. She is the future. Her imagination will shape what comes next. What she thinks is important. It doesn't matter what I think. I'm old. What I think isn't important. It won't *shape* anything it will just float about a bit and if it lands, form a thin unwanted coat, like dust.

MILLIE: You're not that old.

LYN: Of course I am.

MILLIE: You're not, you just look it.

LYN: Why thank you.

MILLIE: I mean the way you speak and stuff, you sound quite young, for a grandma.

Beat.

ALICE: What do you want to be when you grow up, Millie?

MILLIE: I want to be an old woman. I want to have a hundred and twenty babies and marry myself an old man.

ALICE: Well that's nice

MILLIE: It's a song. What do you want to be when you die?

ALICE: Goodness, um. A cat. Like Cleopatra. You remember Cleo –

LYN: Oh for God's sake of course I do. She died years ago. Cleopatra's already dead. You can't become something that's already dead.

MILLIE becomes transfixed by the turtle.

ALICE: I know that. I'm not stupid you know. I just can't hear properly.

LYN: You are stupid. You always have been.

ALICE: Yes, alright I am stupid but what I'm telling you is that I'm deaf, I'm going deaf.

LYN: You could do a Trial.

ALICE: I haven't got Alzheimer's. I'm just a bit deaf.

LYN: You've had Alzheimer's since you were born. It's not just that they're testing for anyway. They'll take anyone.

ALICE: I've got my grandchildren to look after, haven't I?

MILLIE lifts the tape to get closer. She makes a grab for the turtle, takes it out of the water and clutches it to her chest.

MILLIE: I got it I got it I got him!

ALICE and LYN shriek. An alarm goes off.

SCENE FOUR

GOVERNMENT OFFICE.

A whiteboard. Illustrative diagrams appear throughout as MONROE outlines them on the page.

MONROE, AMANDA, MIKE.

MONROE: It's not going to reduce the space, it's just going to mean the space is re-distributed. The pavement itself remains the same. We put the senior lane on the inside and everyone else continues to walk as normal, on the outside.

Beat.

MIKE: Like a swimming pool

MONROE: Like, yes, like a swimming pool

MIKE: Slow lane, fast lane. Or a motorway

MONROE: Yes, it facilitates overtaking, you see

MIKE: Or an escalator

MONROE: Yes, alright, escalator, yes. Basically, we're adapting a long established practice of prioritisation according to speed differentials – for pedestrians. The effect of the system will be to minimise the impact of the preternaturally slow on the majority and, as importantly, allow old people the freedom to walk as slowly as they please.

Beat.

AMANDA: What about fat people?

MONROE: What about fat people?

MIKE: People who are obese.

MONROE: Obese, alright.

AMANDA: Or disabled people? Wheelchairs? Could they use the lane?

MONROE: Yes people in wheelchairs, of course people in wheelchairs.

AMANDA: Electric wheelchairs?

MIKE: Buggies – what about buggies? You could get knocked over by a buggy. People do. People are. All the time.

AMANDA: Would there be a speed limit?

MONROE: Anything that moves faster than the average pedestrian, obviously, would go in the fast lane. No there wouldn't be a speed limit. It would be a question of judgement.

AMANDA: Not age.

MONROE: Age, yes,

MIKE: And ability.

MONROE: Yes.

Beat.

AMANDA: Because the way it works at the moment

MONROE: It doesn't work, that's the point

AMANDA: The way it works at the moment is that people organise themselves on the pavement intuitively. Small people step aside for larger people, children for adults, women for men, people who aren't in a hurry make way for people who are. It's a status game. And those who claim greater status cling to the inside, which would be your senior lane, forcing others to take the outside, which would be your 'normal' lane.

MONROE: Right.

AMANDA: Who exactly is this for?

MONROE: Look. We've made a promise – we live in the most densely populated country in the developing world. We have an average of four hundred and ninety five people per square mile. We've made a promise to the people of this country that they will be able to walk their pavements again without falling off. The problem of overcrowding isn't just going to go away. We need to set boundaries. We can't stop the elderly from going out but we can minimize the impact of the number of people on the streets with no function, the majority of whom are, as you know, over sixty five.

Beat.

AMANDA: How would you separate one part of the pavement from the other? Would there be a line? Or a sign?

MIKE: No, we can do it without signs. We don't have the budget and anyway people hate street furniture. Just a white line.

MONROE: Red.

MIKE: Red. Or yellow.

MONROE: Yellow line. Red line.

AMANDA: I think it's preposterous.

MONROE: I used to think the length at which you choose to wear your skirt was preposterous but I've got used to it.

AMANDA: I don't see how you can legislate for all old people this way. What's the cut off? What about old people who are fast? Young people who are slow? At what age can you use the lane? What happens when two people are travelling at the same speed in different lanes. How do you indicate that you want to overtake? What did you say about my skirt?

MONROE: Give it time and you'll never remember it was otherwise.

AMANDA: You can't tell people how to walk. Everyone – even ants – ants have a brilliantly organised and instinctive system of getting from one place to another without treading on each other's toes. They don't need rules.

MONROE: Ants don't get old.

Beat. AMANDA gathers up her stuff to go.

Where are you going?

SCENE FIVE

ALICE AND LYN'S HOUSE.

ALICE, knitting. LYN and MILLIE, next to her. DYLAN, on the computer.

LYN: I'm going to Brazil. You can sit there with your knit knit knitting but some of us have places to go, some of us are still ready to strip the light fandango before we shuffle off so don't tell me what to do. We're going to Brazil to see the caiman in its natural habitat.

Beat.

ALICE: How are you getting there?

LYN: Well we're not walking.

ALICE: No, alright then. When?

LYN: I don't know, it's up to whatsisname.

ALICE: Who?

LYN: What?

ALICE: What's his name?

LYN: Who?

ALICE: The person who's organising this trip to Brazil.

LYN: Rob.

ALICE: Robbie.

LYN: Yes alright, Robbie.

ALICE: Our brother. Robbie.

LYN: Yes. Him. Did I tell you I've been diagnosed with this memory disorder?

ALICE: Yes. And did I tell you you can't go abroad because you have to earn *points?*

LYN: Points?

ALICE: Yes, points. You have to look after so many grandchildren, or do so many Trials and then you get –

DYLAN: OH CRAP I got shot.

ALICE: How many lives have you got left?

DYLAN: They're all over the place, man.

ALICE: Stick to your side. If you have to go out in the open

DYLAN: They're *invading*.

ALICE: Just keep your finger pressed on the kill button.

LYN: Turn it down, can't you? You're both just as deaf as each other.

Beat.

MILLIE: Robbie said he's going to teach me saxophone. He's busy at the moment but he's going to give me lessons when he's got time.

ALICE: Oh he's very good you know.

MILLIE: I know, I heard him, he's sick.

DYLAN: Yeah well he's working, you know, so.

MILLIE: I know, I just said that. When he finishes filming.

DYLAN: And after that he's going on tour.

MILLIE: Well alright then, when he stops.

DYLAN: He never stops. He says, if he ever stops, he'll die.

LYN: He'll have to soon.

DYLAN: Why?

LYN: How old do you think he is exactly?

DYLAN: I know how old he is.

LYN: No you don't.

DYLAN: I do.

ALICE: Lyn, don't.

DYLAN: He's sixty something.

LYN: Go on. You guess.

MILLIE: Me?

ALICE: *Lyn.*

LYN: How old does he look to you?

MILLIE: I don't know, he's quite young for his age, isn't he, I mean it depends, on his age, obviously, I don't know.

LYN: Have a guess.

ALICE: *Stop it, Lyn.*

MILLIE: Well I thought he was about sixty two.

LYN: He was.

 Beat.

MILLIE: When?

 LYN attempts the calculation

ALICE: Lyn. I'm running out of blue. Would you?

LYN: What?

ALICE: The blue. Could you get me another ball?

LYN: Why don't you? I'm settled.

ALICE: My leg. Please, Lyn. I'll lose the shape.

LYN: Dylan can go.

DYLAN: I have to finish this game.

LYN: You don't *have* to finish the game.

DYLAN: I don't *have* to get off.

ALICE: He has to finish the game or he won't get to the next level.

MILLIE: I'll go. *(MILLIE gets up.)*

DYLAN: Yeah, she can get it.

MILLIE: Shuttup Dylan.

ALICE: You don't know where it is.

LYN: We can give her directions. You know the cupboard upstairs?

MILLIE: Which one?

LYN: You know, the one with the little cocky arms.

MILLIE: Arms?

LYN: Yes, you know, little cocky cocker

ALICE: Copper.

LYN: Arms.

ALICE: Handles.

Beat.

MILLIE: No.

ALICE: Lyn.

LYN: Fine. I'll go.

LYN exits.

LYN: It's your bloody knitting!

Silence.

ALICE: She hasn't always been like this you know.

MILLIE: Like what?

ALICE: Like a child.

MILLIE: She's cool.

DYLAN: What's going to happen?

ALICE: She'll have to do a Trial.

MILLIE: Can't we look after her?

ALICE: No.

DYLAN: Yeah but what's going to happen then?

ALICE: What do you mean?

DYLAN: *(gesturing to MILLIE.)* Well Turtlesnatcher can't stay here.

ALICE: Dylan!

DYLAN: Well she can't, can she, it's against the rules.

ALICE: Of course she can.

DYLAN: No I'm just saying. You're not her Nan. Aunty Lyn is.

ALICE: She's part of our family now, Dylan.

MILLIE: If Nan gets worse

ALICE: She will

MILLIE: When she gets worse. We can look after her ourselves.

ALICE: We can't, Millie. We're not allowed.

MILLIE: We can.

ALICE: No we can't.

MILLIE: I can.

Beat.

DYLAN: So can I. I'm pretty independent for my age. As long as someone else does the cooking. *(Beat.)* And washing. *(Beat.)* And clearing up and stuff.

ALICE: If you can't look after your grandchildren you have to do a Trial and if you've got dementia you go to the front of the queue. She'll be fine.

LYN enters. She looks surprised to see them.

ALICE: You find it?

LYN: What?

ALICE: The wool.

LYN: What wool?

ALICE: The wool you very kindly went upstairs to get for me.

LYN: No. It's got nothing to do with wool. I was upstairs. About to brush my hair. And I realised I'd lost that thing with the you know, I must have put it down somewhere, god only knows, it's completely disappeared. And now you're all here and I haven't even brushed my hair.

Pause.

ALICE: You went upstairs, Lyn, to get my wool.

LYN: Did I? I keep – oh this is awful. Did I tell you I've been diagnosed with this memory thing?

ALICE: Yes.

Pause.

MILLIE: Shall I help you find it, Nan?

LYN: What?

MILLIE: The thing you were looking for.

LYN: Oh yes, darling, would you?

MILLIE: What is it?

LYN: Um.

MILLIE: When did you last see it?

LYN: I put it down and now it's gone.

MILLIE: Is it small or large?

LYN: What?

MILLIE: The thing you're looking for.

LYN: Oh yes I think it must be quite small.

MILLIE: Right.

   Beat.

DYLAN: Is it made of glass or wood or what?

LYN: Base metal.

DYLAN: Metal?

LYN: Yes, I think it's embossed.

DYLAN: In where?

LYN: Well if I knew that we wouldn't be looking would we?

MILLIE: Is it precious?

LYN: I should think so.

DYLAN: Where do you keep your precious stuff? Normally?

LYN: *(She stops in front of the computer screen now, transfixed.)*
   There's a young man pointing a gun at me.

DYLAN: You have to duck down.

   LYN ducks. The firing sound continues.

DYLAN: Do you want a go?

LYN: Do I have to fight?

DYLAN: Yes otherwise you get killed.

LYN: How do you know who's on your side?

DYLAN: Well if they're shooting you

LYN: He's shooting me. Why's he shooting me? He's the same colour.

DYLAN: He's infiltrated. You have to be careful of them. They look the same but see, they're different.

LYN: So who's the enemy?

DYLAN: *My* enemy is the republic of Mikistan. But you can choose. Who would you like your enemy to be?

LYN: My enemy. Is the woman in the bread shop who spits on my doughnuts.

DYLAN: It could be you versus zeds or the blue warriors against the narks. Who do you think would make a good enemy?

LYN: How do I know? Don't ask me.

SCENE SIX

THE OFFICE.

MONROE, AMANDA, MIKE. AMANDA is wearing a skirt down to her ankles.

MONROE: Ask them. Ask all those patients who have shown quantifiable memory improvement within the first three months of Trials. don't ask me. Ask them if the risk is too great. In the Ark alone there are many many – numerous

MIKE: Seventy five patients.

MONROE: Seventy five patients who've recovered – and some of them *discovered* – abilities they didn't even know they had. I see no reason to suspend the drug just because a few relatives have complained of the occasional side effect.

AMANDA: Death, I would have thought, is rather a major side effect.

MONROE: Death, Amanda, is a fact of life. No-one has died from Ryanol.

AMANDA: Fifty four percent of our patients have died within the first four months of admission.

MONROE: They're old. Forty six percent haven't.

AMANDA: After suffering paralysis.

MONROE: Temporary.

MIKE: The majority do tend to recover.

AMANDA: Experiencing severe loss of balance.

MIKE: Sixty three percent.

AMANDA: Headaches, insomnia, low blood pressure and incontinence.

MONROE: But in the process a significant percentage of these people are recorded as having experienced total recall.

MIKE: That's a *hundred percent*.

AMANDA: I know what total means, Mike. But why would anyone want to remember everything?

MONROE: Look.

AMANDA: All I'm saying. The Trials are taken from a position of genuine equipoise and we should wait for all the results before we can be a hundred percent sure that Ryanol is our best option.

MONROE: The only people in this world who are a hundred percent sure about anything are mad. These are *trials*.

AMANDA: Exactly and they're still collating the data from all the rcts.

MONROE: What with? Teaspoons? We have a meeting with the investors –

AMANDA: What about Lazaran?

MIKE: There's no competition. The word is it's improvement over placebo doesn't reach significance.

MONROE: Useless then.

AMANDA: Not useless. Harmless.

MONROE: We can't afford to be harmless.

MIKE: Can I just? *(No-one interrupts.)* We do have a meeting with the investors in twenty four days and they'll want to know whether or not we're pleased with the results on Ryanol. And if we are pleased with the results then we have permission from NICE to roll it out across the whole country.

AMANDA: And if we're not?

MIKE: Then they'll withdraw their funding. *(Beat.)* And take the entire British Stock market down with it.

Beat.

MONROE: Again.

MIKE: Again.

Beat.

AMANDA: The thing is. It's the placebos which are showing the most positive results so far. The pink pills. If you look, there, you'll see there's a ten percent improvement rating in their group.

Beat.

MIKE: How come?

AMANDA: Time and food. Each individual was given an extra fifteen minutes for every appointment. And the ones who ate well, you know, fish oil, vegetables, pulses, etcetera, showed arrested levels of amyloid protein and even demonstrated signs of improvement.

Beat.

MONROE: Oh well bring back leeches why don't we?

AMANDA: Sorry?

MONROE: Let's drink bat's blood and pull toenails off monkeys. This isn't *science*. We're supposed to be collating research not writing a book of recipes. *(Beat.)* I'm sorry

AMANDA: Right.

MONROE: But are you seriously suggesting we forget the drugs and give everyone mung beans instead?

Beat.

AMANDA: Are you angry because it might be a cure or because it obviously isn't?

MONROE: Look, Amanda. What exactly is it, apart from my resignation, that you want? Because it's hard enough trying to keep the bloody purse holders on board without having to convince members of our own committee.

AMANDA: I didn't ask for your resignation. I just made a complaint.

Silence.

MIKE: Can I just? *(No-one interrupts.)* Two things really. Financially speaking I'm not sure the food findings are of great significance. Unless we decide to go into catering. Ha ha. Placebos on the other hand are cheap.

AMANDA: I'm sorry, it's just I think the palliative research is as important as the curative. I'm not saying we should suspend the Trials or anything. I just think Ryanol should go back to the lab before the next stage.

Beat.

MONROE: Your opinions will be noted.

Beat.

AMANDA: Right.

Beat.

MONROE: And how are the fruits of your labour?

AMANDA: Sorry?

MONROE: Robot.

MIKE: Oh it's incredible. I saw the prototype yesterday.

MONROE: Good. I look forward to seeing it.

AMANDA: Her.

Beat.

MONROE: Her.

SCENE SEVEN

CATHY, ALICE, ROBBIE and DYLAN. DYLAN'S on the computer, listening to music. ROBBIE'S hair is now very blond.

CATHY: She has not got Alzheimer's.

ALICE: She has.

CATHY: She can't have. It's an act.

ALICE: She kissed the postman on Tuesday. She kissed the postman and invited him in for tea.

CATHY: Friendliness doesn't denote Alzheimer's.

ALICE: She thought he was Robbie.

ROBBIE: She never kisses me.

ALICE: She talks to her handbag. Every time the phone rings she runs to comfort it because she thinks it's an animal in distress. She forgets what she's doing, who she is, who I am, I can't bear it.

CATHY: Look. This is a woman with a degree in genetic engineering. She's written for the New Scientist. She reads newspapers, novels, she's given lectures. She's been on University Challenge. She can't have Alzheimer's. Not now. Not *yet*. She's too… young. *(Beat.)* She'll have to do a Trial.

ROBBIE: I wouldn't go near the Ark if you paid me.

ALICE: She'll have to and they do pay you.

ROBBIE: They don't pay you. They just don't charge you.

ALICE: They're not a bad thing. People are queuing to get in. You get clean sheets. Food on demand. Company. Entertainment. They have shows you know. It's a touring venue for the RSC. Part of their treatment. Culture.

ROBBIE: Maybe she's pretending.

CATHY: She hates Shakespeare.

ALICE: She's not pretending.

DYLAN: *(Loud. Without taking off his headphones.)* Children are the best medicine.

CATHY: You what?

DYLAN: She has her granddaughter to look after now. That'll sort her out.

CATHY: How's that, Dylan?

ALICE: It's true, they do. They make you forget yourself.

CATHY: That's her problem, Alice.

ALICE: You know what I mean.

DYLAN: Having children makes you less selfish.

CATHY: It doesn't make you less selfish, it just widens the sphere of your selfishness. I haven't noticed that people with children are any nicer than people without.

ROBBIE: Is she with Millie now?

ALICE: I don't know. I hope so. I told you, she just disappears, I have no idea where she goes because when she comes back she can't remember.

DYLAN: Maybe she's been abducted.

CATHY: People don't abduct old women.

DYLAN: By Millie.

CATHY: Don't be silly, Dylan. Why would Millie want to do that?

DYLAN: *Because she knows you want to send her away.*

Pause.

CATHY: Why don't you get off that thing, Dylan? Why don't you get off that thing and do something with your frontal lobe? Every time I come here he just sits there, spending all his time passively absorbing and manipulating stereotypically negative images of mankind in impossibly violent situations. As if there's nothing else to do.

DYLAN: I'm listening to music! And you shouldn't talk about me like I'm not here, Aunty, it's rude.

CATHY: You're not here. You're in your own little world.

DYLAN: We're all in our own little world.

Silence.

CATHY: I know what you're thinking. I know what you're all thinking. But I can't. You know what she's like. She's not *domesticated.* She's a wild ferret, snuffling about, always looking, just waiting to shoot up your leg and bite your head off. I mean I know you have to put up with her, Alice, I know, I'm sorry but she's your sister, you can ignore her, she can ignore you, you can let each other be, and I'm not saying I'm so good to live with myself, I know that, but I don't ask anyone to live with me, I'm alright on my own, I like it on my own, she likes it on her own, if she lived with me, if she came to live with me – I'm sorry, I'm not a child any more – she never even wanted to be a mother and I certainly don't want I can't be a mother not now, god, not to her not like this, I just, it's not that I don't care, it's just, it's not that I don't love her, it's just I'm too young to die I'd rather kill myself.

Silence.

ROBBIE: I don't think that's what any of us were thinking Cathy.

ALICE: She's past that stage.

Beat.

DYLAN: *(Taking off his headphones.)* But we have to decide what to do about Millie.

Beat.

ALICE: I can look after her.

ROBBIE: No, Alice, you've got enough on your plate.

DYLAN: Thanks.

ROBBIE: I don't mean you. I mean, you've already got three and anyway you're not allowed.

CATHY: It's only meant to be a temporary thing.

ALICE: What do you mean, temporary? We're all temporary. He's staying here while his parents get over the birth, she comes here because her mother's working and she hasn't got anyone else. We can't just give her up when we feel like it.

DYLAN: *(To ROBBIE.)* You could look after her. You could be her grandfather.

ROBBIE: Hang on. I'm happy to teach her the saxophone and things. But I'm still working aren't I? I can't.

ALICE: Yes. Robbie's still working.

ROBBIE: Look at my schedule. We're filming in Leeds all week. Friday I've got an audition. Next week it's night shoots. I *work,* you know.

DYLAN: But you're not working all the time, are you?

ALICE drops her wool. She bends down to pick it up and her knee gives way.

ROBBIE: That's not the point. I mean, *yes,* actually, I get a lot of work considering – The point is you can't adopt unless you're over, you know, working age. And I'm not.

DYLAN: Well she can hang out with me.

ROBBIE: She can *hang out* with all of us. But as far as the rules are concerned none of us are suitable to be full time proper paid up grandparents. I'd love to, but, we're all busy.

Beat.

CATHY: Uncle Robbie.

ROBBIE: Yes.

CATHY: Your hair.

ROBBIE: Do you like it?

CATHY: Yes, I – *(Beat.)* Yes.

ROBBIE: Thank you.

DYLAN: He's got a new girlfriend.

CATHY: Mo?

ROBBIE: Chiara. That was months ago.

DYLAN: Pay attention, Aunty.

ROBBIE: Yeah, keep up.

DYLAN: This one works for a charity, she's got blonde wavy hair, big knockers, and she's really old, like forty five.

CATHY: Robbie.

ROBBIE: I didn't say that I did not say that.

DYLAN: No but she has though I've seen a picture.

ROBBIE: It's his interpretation. I can't be held responsible for his interpretation. What are you doing, Alice?

ROBBIE notices ALICE on the floor. She's been trying to get up but is stuck in a kneeling position.

CATHY: What is it?

ALICE: Nothing.

DYLAN: What's happened?

ALICE: I'm just looking. At these wires.

ROBBIE: Why?

ALICE: Just checking they're alright.

ROBBIE: They're fine. What's wrong with them?

ALICE: Nothing. They're alright.

CATHY: Do you want a hand?

ALICE: I think I'll just stay here. For a bit.

CATHY: Oh God. Is it your back?

ALICE: No.

CATHY: Leg?

ALICE: I'm fine.

DYLAN: What is it?

CATHY: Alice?

ALICE: Knee.

CATHY: Would it be better if you sat?

ROBBIE: No.

DYLAN: You shouldn't move them. If they're injured. You shouldn't move them.

ALICE: You carry on. I'll be alright in a minute. Just ignore me.

CATHY: Do you want a a a

DYLAN: Ambulance?

CATHY: Cushion or something?

ROBBIE: Just stay there. Stay there and we'll get you a drink.

DYLAN: Shall we get an ambulance?

ROBBIE: Would you like a drink?

CATHY: Yes. I'll get some water.

ALICE: If you like.

ROBBIE: Whisky?

CATHY goes to fetch some water. There's a glass on the table by the computer. As she leans down to pick it up she knocks the mouse and the screen comes to. Images of LYN, brandishing an arsenal of weapons.

DYLAN: We should call an ambulance.

ROBBIE: Just breathe deeply, Alice. Remember to breathe.

ALICE: I'm really perfectly comfortable here. You all just carry on with what you were doing and I'll be fine.

CATHY: What the hell is this?

ROBBIE squeezes ALICE's knee.

ROBBIE: Can you feel that?

ALICE: What?

DYLAN: I'm gonna call an ambulance.

ROBBIE: I don't need an ambulance. Will you stop – we don't want an ambulance in this house, alright?

Beat.

DYLAN: Alright.

CATHY is transfixed by the computer game.

Onscreen: LYN cruises a large white corridor in a buggy. Two doctors pass, wearing operating masks. She turns, points her umbrella and riddles them with bullets.

Other old people appear in the corridors and rooms. They're fit and upright, but when the enemy appears they feign weakness and start leaning on their sticks, frames and taking to their buggies and beds; the trick is to lure the Medics into combat by eliciting sympathy.

An old man criss crosses the corridor, stealthily. A nurse walks past. He apparently collapses. The nurse turns and approaches him. She produces a syringe. He grabs the syringe, wrestles it from her and injects her.

LYN has an injured arm. She opens a door onto a roomful of Medics and retreats quickly. Too late. They're all out in the corridor. She makes for the nearest ward, dives under the covers of an empty bed, and disguises herself amongst the patients. The Medics enter.

LYN emerges from under the covers with a new re-enforced arm, capable of firing up to 100 metres. There is ducking and diving and shooting and amputation on both sides until a full-scale battle ensues between the Elderly and the Medics. The bodies of both lie scattered, each looting the other for limbs with which to replace their own.

ALICE is left by the others to recover and stand, slowly, in real time, as:

MIMI, the robot, walks into the next scene.

SCENE EIGHT

MONROE, AMANDA and MIKE.

MIMI, the robot, stands before them.

MONROE: And she talks?

AMANDA: Yes, she can talk. She won't be able to expound on the theory of quantum mechanics but she can certainly manage a conversation. Can't you, Mimi?

AMANDA turns to MIMI. MIMI speaks quietly and always with a slight delay.

MIMI: I can.

AMANDA: How are you today, Mimi?

MIMI: I'm fine today. *(Beat.)* And you?

MONROE: She seems to actually follow what you're saying.

AMANDA: She makes eye contact through sensing the direction of the human voice.

MONROE: Hello.

MIMI: Hello.

MONROE laughs. MIMI laughs.

MONROE: She has a sense of humour?

AMANDA: Not as such. She's just reacting to your tone.

MIKE: Does she really understand what we're saying?

AMANDA: Intellectually, no. Empathetically, yes.

MONROE: Extraordinary.

MIKE: Told you.

MONROE: So. If I were a patient?

AMANDA: Well we all know about the therapeutic effect of pets. When you stroke a cat the cat purrs and this in itself is a reward. Well Mimi's function is identical. Her response (and she is essentially reactive) serves to press certain Darwinian buttons in the patient which convince them that they're in a relationship with her. She reflects the patient's emotions back to themselves and in so doing helps them deal with them.

MONROE: Right.

AMANDA: And of course, she responds physically, like a pet, to being stroked.

Beat.

MONROE: Where?

AMANDA: Anywhere you like.

MONROE: Here?

AMANDA: Go on. She won't bite.

MONROE strokes her arm. She 'purrs' in response.

MIKE: I think she likes you.

AMANDA: Her states of mind are affected by how she's treated. For example, is she stroked gently or aggressively? If she's provoked physically she'll back away. If she's spoken to angrily she might bristle, as it were, and the patient, you see, would notice this and instinctively take measures to soothe her and in so doing soothe themselves.

MONROE: Very clever.

MIMI: Clever. Thank you.

MONROE: You know who she reminds me of?

MIKE: Your dog.

MONROE: Ffion.

MIKE: His dog.

MONROE: Incredible.

MIKE: Isn't it? I mean, do you have to be ill to get one? Haha.

Beat.

MONROE: Are we on target for the launch?

MIKE: We're on time, yes. We have slightly gone over budget but it should balance out when you measure it against the staff lay offs.

MONROE: How much?

MIKE: And I was thinking we can always claw something back via the screening campaign.

MONROE: The scans. Were meant to be free.

MIKE: *Were,* yes.

MONROE: 'Free at the point of service'. I mean why would anyone want to pay to find out something they don't want to know?

MIKE: People like paying. If you make them pay they think it's worth having.

MONROE: We've already made the announcement.

MIKE: I know. It's a bit of a pr balls up, but we could get Amanda to launch the campaign along with the robot. We need to reach as wide a demographic as possible.

MONROE: No we don't. We need to reach *old* people.

MIKE: But no because it's detectable much earlier isn't it? As I understand it the scans can predict neurological disorders a long time before they actually happen. They might show up five years before, they might show up fifty years before, who knows, we don't know yet, it's not a science.

AMANDA: Yes, Mike, it is. It's detectable fifteen-twenty years in advance.

MIKE: At the moment, maybe –

AMANDA: So there's no point in anyone below the age of forty having a scan.

MONROE: And I really don't see why I should stand up there and ask the public to bail us out because we've gone over on the bloody robot.

He gestures aggressively to MIMI. She backs off and squawks in response.

MONROE: Sorry.

AMANDA: She's okay.

MIMI: Sorry.

AMANDA: You okay?

MIMI: I'm okay.

MONROE: Okay.

MIMI: I'm okay. How are you?

MONROE: Fine.

MIMI: Fine. You're cross.

MONROE: I'm not.

MIMI: Don't be cross.

MONROE: *(To AMANDA.)* Can we stop this?

AMANDA strokes MIMI and calms her.

MIKE: We'll have to think of some other way or raising revenue then.

MONROE: And if anybody's going to launch the screening campaign it should be me. We don't want to encourage twenty five year olds to start panicking because they can't remember their mother's maiden name and go round taking up the beds of old people.

AMANDA: I'm not twenty five. But yes, I think you should do the launch. You're more eligible.

MONROE: Thank you. She means old.

AMANDA: I mean old enough.

SCENE NINE

LYN AND ALICE'S HOUSE.

LYN, ROBBIE, CATHY and MILLIE. ROBBIE'S wearing a leather jacket and has trendy tufted hair. MILLIE is upset but trying to hide it.

CATHY: Why don't you sit down Mum?

LYN: I don't want to sit down. You sit down.

CATHY: We want to talk to you.

LYN: So talk standing up. What are we, Maoris?

ROBBIE: Lyn, sit down. This is important.

She does.

LYN: Alright Mr leather jacket, why don't you take it off if you're staying?

ROBBIE: You like it?

CATHY: He's got a new girlfriend. *(LYN looks at MILLIE, to ROBBIE and back to MILLIE again.)* No not Millie! That's Millie, Mum.

LYN: Where is she then?

CATHY: No, she's not *here.* I was just saying.

LYN: Who's not here?

CATHY: Chiara.

ROBBIE: Rachel.

CATHY: Rachel I mean. Millie wanted to come with us today because – she just wanted –

Beat.

MILLIE: Hello Nan, how are you?

LYN: Hello darling. You've put your hair up. Isn't she lovely?

MILLIE: Thanks.

LYN: Putting on a bit of weight, that's good. Are you still a vegetarian?

ROBBIE: Yes, I'm afraid she is.

MILLIE looks like she might cry.

LYN: *(To MILLIE.)* He doesn't look well though, does he?

ROBBIE: I'm fine Lyn.

LYN: Well why don't you take your coat off if you're staying? (*He does.*) You've got very beautiful eyes. Are you Greek?

Beat.

ROBBIE: Actually her boyfriend is. *(To MILLIE.)* Isn't he?

LYN: Oh how marvellous. What's his name?

MILLIE: Demetrius.

LYN: Demetrius indeed. From Thessalonika?

MILLIE: Yes. My God, do you know him?

LYN: Son of Euthydemus.

MILLIE: No. *(Beat.)* His Mum's Greek, his Dad's from Sweden.

LYN: Have we met?

Beat.

MILLIE: Millie. I'm your –

LYN: Yes yes I know who you are for goodness sake. You're my granddaughter.

CATHY: None of us have met him.

LYN: Who?

CATHY: Her boyfriend. Demetrius.

LYN: Ah. Is he Greek?

CATHY: Yes.

Beat.

LYN: *(To ROBBIE:)* Oh Peter do go and get us some tea would you?

ROBBIE gets up.

ROBBIE: Lyn. We've got to tell you something.

LYN: A secret? I love secrets.

ROBBIE: It's about you and Alice.

LYN: Where *is* Alice?

CATHY: She's had an accident and she's in hospital.

LYN: What kind of accident?

CATHY: Oh you know what she's like. She just tripped over her foot.

LYN: We should go and visit her.

ROBBIE: We've been to visit her, this morning. We've just come back from visiting her.

LYN: No we most certainly did not this morning. It's Tuesday. I was having my hair done. Don't listen to him, he's a nefarious trickster.

ROBBIE: She's in hospital, Lyn.

LYN: We'll have to get her out.

ROBBIE: No, she'll be out any day. Don't worry about Alice. We need to talk about you.

LYN: I'm fine.

ROBBIE: Lyn. You're not.

LYN: Don't tell me what I am and am not. You don't know what I am. You don't know what people are. Look at her! *(Gestures to MILLIE.)* She's supposed to be in love. She's young, beautiful, clever and miserable as winter. I'm perfectly happy as I am thank you so leave me alone.

CATHY: We can't leave you alone, Mum. That's the point.

LYN: Yes you can. We're all alone. We're born alone and we die alone.

Beat.

CATHY: No. We're not.

LYN: Yes we are and that's fine by me.

CATHY: We're born *attached*. We're born *attached* to our mothers.

LYN: We're born, we die –

CATHY: How we die is another question. How we die depends

MILLIE bursts into tears.

LYN: Now look what you've done.

ROBBIE: What is it, Millie?

CATHY: What's the matter?

ROBBIE: You don't have to say if you don't want to.

LYN: What is it?

CATHY: I'm sorry did I? –

LYN: What's going on?

ROBBIE: No she doesn't have to say. You don't have to say anything, Millie.

CATHY: Unless you want to.

MILLIE: *(After a while.)* People trust me. And then they hate me. They tell me their secrets because I can keep a secret, that's why they tell me, but I don't tell them my secrets, so they hate me. And then things change. The secret stays the same and I've still got it but things have changed and they don't feel the same way any more and then they really hate me. *(She cries again.)*

ROBBIE: Nobody hates you. What are you talking about? How can anyone hate you?

LYN: I don't hate you. I think you're lovely.

MILLIE: You don't know what I'm like.

ROBBIE: We do and we're all very fond of you, Millie.

MILLIE: You don't you don't you don't, I'm horrible.

LYN: Who are these people who tell you secrets and hate you? Who are they?

CATHY: Is that what's been bothering you, Millie?

MILLIE: No.

Pause.

LYN: I've got a secret that I'm not going to tell you. *(Beat.)* Have you ever looked at my brother's ears?

MILLIE: What?

CATHY: Mum.

LYN: Here. *(Touches in front of her ear.)* Just round the edges.

CATHY: Don't.

LYN: Bottom of the lobe and just inside the –

CATHY: Stop it. Please listen, Mum. Because you can't stay here on your own any more. They want you to do Trials and they're offering you room, board and everything – it's a nice place, I've seen it.

Beat.

LYN: You killed my cat.

CATHY: I what?

LYN: She killed my cat you know.

CATHY: What cat?

LYN: You went out in the middle of the night to see that
boy. You shouldn't have done that because you hadn't
passed your driving test, had you? No you hadn't. You
took our car, and when you came back, all steamed up
with excitement, when you came back from your lusty
encounter you ran over Cleopatra. She didn't stand a
chance. You could see the tyre marks in the morning all
over her little soft little sweet body. *(She starts to howl.)*
Dead, she's dead, she's all dead.

ROBBIE tries to comfort LYN.

MILLIE: Did you?

CATHY: No I did not.

LYN: Oh yes you did. You murdered her.

CATHY: This is years.

ROBBIE: Sssh, it's alright, come here.

LYN: I saw you at the window. But I didn't want to say
anything because Daddy would have killed you. Her little
black face, all squished.

ROBBIE: Shsh

LYN: And now you want to kill my sister.

ROBBIE: Alice is fine. She's going to be alright.

LYN: I want her back.

CATHY: Don't, please, Mum. This isn't easy.

LYN: She used to like me best. I was the one who chose her.
She was my cat.

CATHY: Mum.

LYN: How could you? How could you you wicked wicked girl!

ROBBIE: Lyn, stop it.

LYN: Murderer! Murderer!

ROBBIE: Right. You can't stay here anymore and that's that. Okay. End of story. In the car, thank you, let's go.

MILLIE: Uncle Robbie.

ROBBIE: It's a strategy. Come on, let's go. Where's your suitcase? *(He moves abruptly and strains his back. He lets out an involuntary yelp.)*

CATHY: Are you alright?

ROBBIE: Fine. Suitcase?

CATHY: Is it your stomach?

ROBBIE: It's nothing. We need to pack a suitcase.

CATHY: Millie, do you know where she keeps her suitcase?

MILLIE doesn't move. She's staring at ROBBIE's ears.

ROBBIE: What?

MILLIE: I was just looking.

ROBBIE: At what?

MILLIE: Your –

CATHY: Suitcase Millie.

LYN: Darling. He's quite a catch isn't he, with his new leather jacket. Mutton dressed as ham. You want to keep your eye on him.

MILLIE: I'm not – tell her, Robbie. Tell her I'm her granddaughter. Tell her who I am.

ROBBIE: *Don't talk about her as if she isn't here.*

Beat.

MILLIE: Did you kill her cat?

CATHY: It was my cat.

ROBBIE takes CATHY in his arms.

ROBBIE: Suitcase. Come on.

ROBBIE and CATHY exit. Silence.

MILLIE: Nan. I'm going to tell you something. And you're going to forget it.

LYN: Is this a magic trick?

MILLIE: It's a secret. Something that's important to me. But not to you.

LYN: Well go on then.

Pause.

MILLIE: I'm pregnant.

LYN: No.

MILLIE: I am pregnant.

LYN: Oh how wonderful.

MILLIE: No no no Nan it's not.

LYN: A baby!

MILLIE: I can't have it.

LYN: Of course you can. I'll look after it.

MILLIE: I'm sixteen, man.

LYN: I'll have it I'll have it.

MILLIE: I'm not going to have it.

LYN: A great grandchild. How marvellous. They'll give me another stipend

MILLIE: No, Nan.

LYN: I'll look after it and you can carry on being sixteen. Who's the father?

MILLIE: Demetrius.

LYN: Who?

MILLIE: It doesn't matter.

LYN: How pregnant?

MILLIE: She'll kill me.

LYN: Who?

MILLIE: My Mum.

LYN: Don't tell her. We won't tell any of them. Sssh. Don't tell anyone else.

MILLIE: *(Laughs.)* You're mad, Nan, you're so mad.

LYN: Our secret.

CATHY and ROBBIE return with a suitcase.

CATHY: What's happened?

MILLIE: Nothing.

CATHY: Why are you laughing?

LYN: She's pregnant!

Beat.

CATHY: Don't be silly, Mum.

LYN: Eight weeks. I'm not.

MILLIE: I didn't tell you that.

LYN: Isn't it wonderful?

CATHY: Oh. God.

LYN: She's not pleased.

ROBBIE: But you're just a *child*.

MILLIE: I'm *sixteen*, uncle Robbie.

ROBBIE: Yes of course you are.

MILLIE: I'm sorry. I'm so sorry.

ROBBIE: No, I – no, that's not the point.

CATHY: Are you… pleased? *(MILLIE shakes her head.)* No, of course you're not. Oh Millie.

MILLIE crawls, crying, onto LYN's lap.

LYN: Why is everyone so miserable? It's a baby. I'll look after it. I told her. I'm good with babies. I'll take care of it. A great wonderful grandchild. *(She picks up a cushion and cradles it.) (Sings.)* Twinkle twinkle little lamb how I wonder what you are…up above the sky so bright, like a diamond in the sky….

END OF ACT ONE

ACT TWO

SCENE ONE

The Hospital. MONROE, AMANDA and MIKE.

A magnified projection of two brains. One is 'normal' the other, MONROE'S, shows up some abnormalities.

(The two hemispheres merge imperceptibly during the scene, and are transformed into the image of a foetus.)

    AMANDA and MIKE study the images.

    Silence.

MIKE: Could it be something else? (*Beat. AMANDA shakes her head.*) Maybe there's been a mix up? (*Beat.*) It could be years. Before it really shows up.

AMANDA: It will be. Twenty years probably, she said.

MIKE: It's very faint.

AMANDA: It is very faint.

MIKE: You'd never know. My grandfather had it for thirty years before it was diagnosed – I mean he was always a bit doolally – but in the end he died in a car crash anyway.

MONROE: It's…

    Beat.

MIKE: Hardly there at all really.

    Silence.

AMANDA: At least you'll be getting the best treatment.

MONROE: What do you mean?

AMANDA: Well. You'd be able to go to the Ark obviously.

MONROE: I'm not going anywhere.

Beat.

AMANDA: Oh.

MONROE: I have no intention of going anywhere.

AMANDA: Not forever, obviously.

MIKE: No need for that.

AMANDA: But you'd want to do a trial.

MONROE: I don't want to do a trial.

Beat.

AMANDA: How. How would we explain that?

MONROE: I'm fifty *three*.

AMANDA: Right.

MONROE: I have no symptoms.

AMANDA: No.

MONROE: And I have a job to do.

AMANDA: Yes.

MONROE: I haven't got *anything*. I might get something in fifteen years. Or twenty years. That's all.

AMANDA: Yes. But if they can catch it early –

MONROE: I'm perfectly healthy. I play tennis twice a week, I eat seeds, my doctor's always congratulating me on my cholesterol levels and I don't go round forgetting my keys. I just have a couple of links missing in my hippocampus. Who hasn't?

AMANDA: I know. It's absurd. Those little red dots.

MONROE: How can they test me? How can they measure my progress if I don't have any symptoms?

AMANDA: *(She gestures to the projected image.)* She said. They track the neural pathways with self assembling wires and measure the levels of pbt6 with the scanner.

Beat.

MONROE: And what about the drugs?

AMANDA: What about the drugs?

MONROE: How could I test the drugs when I know what they are? How can I be an impartial subject?

MIKE: You wouldn't know what they are, would you though? Half the doctors don't know what they are. The tests are double blind.

Beat.

MONROE: I'm not testing Ryanol.

AMANDA: You won't have to.

MONROE: Lazaran, maybe or one of those – why not?

Beat.

AMANDA: Well. They've altered the levels of the cH inhibitor in order to address the side effects. Like we said.

MONROE: I know that.

AMANDA: And now we've got the results

MIKE: Yesterday. You were at the Conference.

AMANDA: Patients still tend to suffer from temporary paralysis and loss of balance but they're recorded as having a huge increase in appetite, energy and sexual impulse. The patients themselves are oblivious to these changes They just say they feel better.

MONROE: Well that's good.

AMANDA: And then they die.

MONROE: What do you mean?

MIKE: After seeing parrots apparently.

AMANDA: Yes. They start hallucinating, always parrots, then they die. It seems the dose required to ameliorate the side effects is lethal.

MIKE: So the Euthanasia society have put in an offer for the lot.

Beat.

MONROE: Well they can't have it. We didn't spend seven years and nine hundred and fifty million pounds in order to produce a cheap suicide pill.

MIKE: It won't be cheap, don't worry. But it'll be a very expensive failure if we don't do something with it.

MONROE: But we can't – we're trying – we were going to –

AMANDA: We're in negotiation.

Beat.

MONROE: I see. *(Beat.)* I'm out of the office five minutes and who's been sitting in my chair?

AMANDA: Sorry?

MONROE: 'Who killed cock robin? Not I said the sparrow with my bow and arrow.'

AMANDA: Why are we doing nursery rhymes?

MONROE: You've been running around my back spreading lies, rumours, sedition, implying that I'm some sort of *misogynist. (To MIKE.)* You know I've been under 'observation' for six months? And now, now you think you've finally got rid of me you dare to look at me with pity. Now you think you're Queen of Hearts it's oh well 'off with his head' and let's sell the bloody tarts and oh look, *(Indicates MIKE.)* says Simple Simon, here comes the pie man, why don't we give him the whole lot for a handful of beans? Brilliant. Old dilly dilly will be halfway down the yellow brick road eating poppies with the munchkins by the time he cottons on. Jesus Christ. If you think I'm giving up on a cure now, if you think we can throw all that research, money, *faith*, down the toilet then you're the one who needs a scan. You're the one who's losing their incy wincy mind. You think you make the decisions here? Well let me tell you something Goldilocks. This is my house, this is my porridge and that's my chair so please don't start re-arranging the furniture yet because I'm not disappearing into the deep dark forest to sleep for a hundred years, I'm just going to speak to the Board.

He picks up his briefcase and goes.

MIKE: He's just upset.

AMANDA: I know.

MIKE: He's right. There is a danger he'll know which drug they're testing. He knows a placebo from the real thing.

AMANDA: Only because placebos are usually pink. We'll just make sure there are no pink pills in his trial.

Beat.

MIKE: God, fifty three.

AMANDA: I *know.*

MIKE picks up the keys on the table.

MIKE: Oh no. Look. He has.

AMANDA: What?

MIKE: He's forgotten his keys.

SCENE TWO

Projection: A scan of the foetus. MILLIE, pregnant.

SCENE THREE

HOSPITAL BED.

LYN, CATHY, MIMI.

LYN: Green duvet, third from the left. Never stops talking. Just rabbiting on and on about who's turned the gas off and she – that one, I don't know what they're all doing in my room – the cow in the corner – hasn't said a word since she came in, just stares at everyone, dull as a box of hair.

CATHY: They can hear you.

LYN: *Good.* These people are mad. Can we go now?

CATHY: No Mum we can't go anywhere. Have you had any breakfast today?

LYN: Cup of tea and a piece of cardboard. Shall I tell you a secret? Shall I?

CATHY: Go on.

LYN: There's a young man. Keeps coming to visit. I think he's taken quite a shine to me. Tall, thin, white jacket.

CATHY: Doctor.

LYN: Reminds me a bit of my husband.

CATHY: Dad.

LYN: What?

CATHY: He was my father.

LYN: No he's not your father don't be ridiculous he's half your age.

CATHY: No. The doctor is like my father.

LYN: That's what I think. It's uncanny, the resemblance, don't you think?

CATHY: I don't know Mum. I haven't met him.

LYN looks at MIMI.

LYN: What is she talking about?

MIMI: Talking. I don't know.

LYN: She understands everything you say you know. Isn't she marvellous?

CATHY: Is she?

LYN: *(Pets MIMI:)* Yes you are, aren't you?

MIMI: I am?

LYN: Yes you are.

MIMI: You are.

MIMI purrs

CATHY: Mum. I need to talk to you about what's going to happen.

LYN: What's going to happen?

CATHY: Well. They're trying out these new drugs to see which ones work best. And then they want to see if they can regulate your neural network, to help your memory, by putting these tiny tiny wires, the size of a hair, into your brain. They're meant to be very effective.

Beat.

LYN: Did I tell you, there's this man. I think he's got a bit of a thing about me. Can't think why, he's half my age and he's really very –

CATHY: Does he remind you of anyone?

LYN: Do you know, he does, yes he does remind me of someone.

CATHY: Dad.

LYN: That's it! He reminds me of Dad. That's exactly it.

CATHY: In what way. Does he remind you of Dad?

LYN: Who?

CATHY: The doctor.

LYN: His head is too big for his body. Always has been. There's nothing you can do about it. I was worried you'd turn out the same but you haven't got a very big head at all. You've got a beautiful head. I'll never forget the first time I cradled it, like a Faberge egg. I keep forgetting things, Cathy, you have no idea. I don't want to forget that.

LYN starts to stroke MIMI unconsciously. MIMI makes mewling noises.

CATHY: Mum. *(Beat.)* Mum. There's something I wanted to ask you about Dad. It's probably nothing. But I've always wondered. There was this woman. Odette. I came across her in some photos the other day. She used to come to the house now and then. *(She puts her hand on MIMI's arm.)* Could you stop doing that now please? *(MIMI is stricken. She stops stroking LYN's arm.)* Thank you. She was a work colleague of Dad's and her name was Odette.

LYN: Odille.

CATHY: That's it. Odille. I must have been about eight or nine. He would have met her in France in that period when he was working a lot in France. And when she came for dinner oh it was probably nothing, it's just I can't help thinking about it, I have this memory of them laughing and of you not laughing and then her having to leave suddenly and us eating dinner in silence and I've always wondered or rather I've only just realised I've always wondered. Were they having an affair?

LYN: France?

CATHY: Yes, when he went away to France.

LYN: He would never have gone to France. Not as far as I know. Not willingly.

CATHY: It was with work, Mum.

LYN: I had a French friend once, but she turned. It's a well known fact, you know. They can't stand us. The French.

CATHY: You're half French. Your Dad, remember?

LYN: Quite. Couldn't stand any of us when it came down to it. I caught him sticking pins in my effigy once.

CATHY: No, Mum, you did not. I want to know. Did my father –

LYN: Don't you tell me what I did and didn't do. I did I tell you I most certainly did. You see. *(To MIMI:)* This is what I have to put up with. All the time. No you didn't yes you did. I've had enough. You come here and you insult me and blame me for everything – it's not my fault. It's not my fault you never had children. *(She gets up and starts to march out.)* I don't have time to listen to your stories. I have to meet Diana by the canal in half an hour so you can just stay here and think about what you've said. I will not be treated like this any more. Don't even think of following me.

She goes. CATHY looks at MIMI. MIMI returns the look.

CATHY: Shouldn't you go after her?

MIMI: Shouldn't you go after her?

CATHY stares at MIMI. MIMI shudders. Silence.

LYN returns. She sits down warily.

LYN: *(to CATHY:)* Tell me. Have we had a disagreement? I feel like I've had a disagreement but I'm not sure who with. Is it with Alice? I don't know what's happened to her? I haven't seen her for ages.

Have we had an argument?

CATHY: No. She fell over, remember.

LYN: Yes I know that but where is she?

CATHY: Same place as you but round the corner. You're both staying here for now.

LYN: Don't be ridiculous. I'm not staying here.

CATHY: Mum.

LYN: *(Shrill.)* I'm not staying *here*.

MIMI whines in alarm.

LYN: How could you?

CATHY: It's alright, please don't Mum, it's alright, they'll look after you.

LYN: How could you how could you *(To MIMI.)* how could they?! *(MIMI whines. LYN puts out her hand. MIMI takes it, strokes it and purrs.)* How could they throw me to the wolves? You see what they're like?

MIMI: It's alright, Lyn, it's alright.

LYN: Throw me to the wolves.

MIMI: Don't be upset.

LYN: I am upset, I'm traumatised.

MIMI: Traumatised.

LYN: I feel

MIMI: Feel sad.

LYN: Yes, sad.

MIMI: You feel sad. I feel sad.

LYN strokes MIMI's hand. MIMI purrs.

LYN: Don't be sad.

MIMI: Poor Lyn.

LYN: I know, I know.

MIMI: We're sad.

LYN: You mustn't be sad.

MIMI: We mustn't be sad.

LYN: We're not sad, are we?

MIMI: We're not sad.

LYN: No. *(LYN continues stroking MIMI's arm.)* Is that better?

MIMI: That's better.

SCENE FOUR

THE OFFICE.

AMANDA and MIKE.

    AMANDA, in MONROE'S chair.

AMANDA: It's a *nightmare.*

MIKE: Who did you speak to? They can't change their minds. Why have they changed their minds?

AMANDA: They've tested it. I spoke to Mr Euthanasia himself. They've tested it and they say it's painless, yes, pleasurable even –

MIKE: The hallucinations

AMANDA: Parrots and all that, yes. But not, as befits their purpose, instant.

MIKE: So. It's just taking people too long

AMANDA: To die.

MIKE: But. We just can't afford a marketplace loss that size. We have to keep the drug in rotation.

AMANDA: And now the Board are complaining.

MIKE: What of?

AMANDA: The numbers.

MIKE: What numbers? The numbers are fine. They're hardly on the street any more. Elderly traffic is down fifteen percent on last quarter.

AMANDA: The numbers *inside*. Because they're not getting better. They're getting sicker and older and the palliative care is so good they don't want to leave and they can't leave anyway because the Trials are making them sicker so the Ark is fit to bust and all we've produced is some high class poison.

Beat.

MIKE: The helmets are showing good results.

AMANDA: Long term memory, yes. Short term, no.

Beat.

MIKE: But. The palliative area is going well.

AMANDA: What we really need, to make any significant breakthrough, is more brains.

MIKE: Too well, some might say. Palliative Care. Like a bottle neck.

AMANDA: For some reason people are squeamish about leaving them behind. They'll leave their kidneys, livers, lungs without a second thought. But not their brains. If we can just persuade them during the Trials to part with their brains at the end.

Beat.

MIKE: Of the Trials?

AMANDA: Of their *life.*

MIKE: Of course. *(Beat.)* Can I just? *(AMANDA doesn't interrupt.)*

AMANDA: *What?*

MIKE: If there was a solution which made them *feel* better –

AMANDA: Ryanol will never be a cure, Mike.

MIKE: But actually made them worse? I didn't say cure. I said solution.

Beat.

AMANDA: What do you mean?

MIKE: I mean something with a…dual function.

AMANDA: What? Like –

MIKE: I mean if there was a drug.

AMANDA: Yes.

MIKE: Which gave them pleasure, let's say.

AMANDA: Right.

MIKE: But which also speeded up the pace … which somehow accelerated their actual …

AMANDA: Deterioration?

MIKE: Exactly. It's a deterioration. Nobody wants to prolong it, do they?

AMANDA: No.

Beat.

MIKE: It would be a kindness, wouldn't it?

Beat.

AMANDA: Who for?

MIKE: Those, for example, who've already done the Trials.

AMANDA: You mean –

MIKE: I mean those who can't be helped.

AMANDA: The ones who –

MIKE: The ones who are too far gone.

AMANDA: Right.

MIKE: Do you see?

AMANDA: To give them some quality of life before the end.

MIKE: For them to have a sense of heightened wellbeing before they die. Would be a good thing.

Beat.

AMANDA: Would they know?

MIKE: Know what?

AMANDA: What they were choosing?

MIKE: Oh they'd have a choice, yes. If they choose quality of life over cure. Quality of life has always been an option.

AMANDA: The only difference being

MIKE: That instead of the old pink placebo

AMANDA: They'd get Ryanol.

MIKE: Which would guarantee both pleasure / and death.

AMANDA: And death.

MIKE: The quality of life pill.

AMANDA: And the choice would be open to anyone …in that category?

MIKE: It would be up to the consultants to select the most appropriate and deserving.

AMANDA: Of course.

Beat.

MIKE: Although I think it's fairly obvious, isn't it, when someone has lost touch with reality?

SCENE FIVE

HOSPITAL WARD.

> *ALICE, in bed. DYLAN, beside her. LYN, pacing. She's wearing a memory aid contraption on her head with spokes sticking out of it.*

LYN: There's the yellow crazy ant it's called *anoplolepis gracilipes* and what they do they kill red crabs on Christmas Island and generally destroy the ecosystem for the other seventeen species of crab found there including the *coconut crab* which is as we all know is the largest terrestrial invertebrate in the known world. Yuk. Mummy was a terrible cook let's be honest ha your face look at you it's only liver and onions *only only* who'd want to eat someone's liver indeed now you've spilt gravy all down your front, silly, you're going to have to change in order for things to stay the same in order for things to stay the same in order *(A moment. She adjust one of the spokes in her head.)* oh Daddy was a fine one to talk just sitting on the dock of the bay watching the tide come in oh yes I've been in a boat I've been in boats many times what kind of boat topaz schooner finn catamaran not in the water mind oh look there's smoke coming out of the house window fridge

DYLAN: Chimney.

LYN: Chimney – there's smoke coming out of the chimney I think correct me if I'm wrong but I think we are being watched, young man.

DYLAN: We are.

ALICE: Dylan.

LYN: *(To ALICE.)* Oh it's your own fault if you will put your hand down the well it's no wonder the wasps stung you Mummy's trying to catch you but you're faster than her I can hear her oh what a terrible terrible oh *(She puts her hands over her ears and rocks.)*

DYLAN: What can you hear?

LYN: Screaming like a monkey she's shouting you're screaming what a pair I'm off down the hill through the Cyprus fig in Italy / yes *trees* treading on all

DYLAN: Trees

LYN: Those infernal rockets.. that's not right.

DYLAN: Rockets?

LYN: Lettuces! I can hardly breathe however fast I run I can still hear her, I can feel those evil wasps in my ear

DYLAN: Don't look back.

LYN: I'm not looking back

DYLAN: Try and find some shelter. You see any shelter?

LYN: I can see a little pink house through the trees and a swimming pool I didn't even know was there.

DYLAN: Go for it.

LYN: Two children, one skinny with blue trunks, the other a strapping toddler – Sasha her name is! – with a flowery hat jumping up and down

DYLAN: Are they safe?

LYN: They're safe.

DYLAN: Go on then. Advance with caution. Have you got any ammo?

LYN: Oh dear I've left my umbrella behind I knew there was something trees release volatiles you know that warn their neighbours that gypsy moth larvae are attacking their leaves but Heloise will get it. Off you go.

ALICE: Alice.

LYN: Alice. Silly cow, I've always had a terrible memory for names. I know, you're my sister, I know that. And Robbie's my brother. Where is he? I last saw him playing in the garage with his airfix. Panzer division against the 3rd battalion I accidentally squashed a whole section of the rearguard you know – well they were hidden in a mound of mud it's not my fault. But you're the favourite with your pigtails and your dimples I'm not surprised you always do the washing up and he never wanted a girl second time round anyway so he tried to strangle me at birth but Doctor Simkins walked in on her and it's not your fault you're perfect Jesus Christ where's your leg?

ALICE: I fell over didn't I?

LYN: I know that I know that but what have they done with your leg?

ALICE: It was no good, Lyn, they had to take it off.

LYN: It has it's gone!

ALICE: No good to man nor beast.

LYN: But. There was nothing wrong with it.

ALICE: Oh yes there was. Severe nerve damage.

LYN: But they didn't have to do that.

ALICE: It's the diabetes. They did. It doesn't matter.

LYN: But it was *your* leg.

ALICE: Oh stop it.

LYN: Stop it yourself. You're talking rubbish.

DYLAN: They can't just cut off your leg.

ALICE: Well I didn't want the pills. They taste horrid and there's no guarantee. It was the easier option all round. Anyway haven't you heard of stem cells? They can help grow things back you know.

LYN: Don't be stupid.

ALICE: I am not being stupid. Will you stop – I'm sick of people calling me stupid.

DYLAN: But Nan. You can't. Grow another leg.

ALICE: Well we'll see about that. If I do I do, if I don't it doesn't matter it was no good anyway. I'm helping them with their research.

DYLAN: I'm telling Robbie.

ALICE: Oh there's too much fuss made about bodies. In a hundred years everyone will understand that bodies are just bodies and there's no such thing as death.

LYN: You're mad.

ALICE: No Lyn, you're mad.

ROBBIE enters, ashen.

DYLAN: Uncle Robbie. Have you seen about Nan's leg. It's gone!

Beat.

ROBBIE: Yes.

DYLAN: What did he say?

ROBBIE: Who?

DYLAN: The doctor.

ROBBIE: Nothing.

DYLAN: What do you mean, *nothing?*

ROBBIE: I mean *nothing.*

DYLAN: Oh where is the bloody doctor? This is *appalling!*

ROBBIE: The bloody doctor – don't swear, Dylan. He – she – I couldn't find her. Let's go. Come on.

DYLAN: We've only just got here.

ROBBIE: You're upset.

DYLAN: I'm not upset. I'm *angry*. You're upset.

ROBBIE: I'm not upset.

DYLAN: Yes you are. You're not looking at me.

ROBBIE: I am not. You are. We should go.

LYN: Are we going? Well that's marvellous, but I haven't packed yet. Let me go and pack. I've got a few letters of complaint to write about the standard of food in this hotel I can tell you. I'll be glad to see the back of this place. Only thing I'll miss is the sex.

She goes.

DYLAN: Did she say sex? *(Beat.)* Why did she say sex?

ROBBIE: No idea.

ALICE: She doesn't even like it. It's like pantomime, she used to say. Silly and rude, but atleast it's only once a year.

ROBBIE: She must have meant something else.

DYLAN: Maybe she meant drugs.

Beat.

ROBBIE: Come on. Leave your Nan in peace now.

DYLAN: What did the doctor say?

ROBBIE: I told you. I didn't see the doctor.

DYLAN: What did you see then?

ROBBIE: Nothing.

DYLAN: Nothing?

ROBBIE: Yes, Dylan. Nothing.

DYLAN: Don't believe you. You're such a bad actor.

ROBBIE: I saw no-one. Nothing. Just empty beds. Ward after ward. Vacant corridors. Total silence.

Beat.

DYLAN: Then what?

ROBBIE: Then. *(Beat.)* A room at the end of the corridor. Muffled scrabbling noises coming from inside. There was a sign on the door. Only the letters M. R. and G. were left.

DYLAN: Mr G?

ROBBIE: And the sound of an incinerator.

DYLAN: What sound does an incinerator make?

ROBBIE makes a series of churning and humming noises.

DYLAN: *(DYLAN rolls his eyes.)* Oh man. Your stories are so crap, Uncle Robbie. *(The message tone goes on DYLAN's phone. He puts his earphones on to listen and walks away.)*

Silence.

ROBBIE: Alice. *(He checks that DYLAN's not listening.)* The doctor said. You're responding well to your treatment. But she said. You're an interesting case. And they want. They want to take one of you're your…

ALICE: Distal phalanges, yes, I know.

ROBBIE: Fingers.

ALICE: Just one.

ROBBIE: I said they couldn't.

ALICE: It's only the tip.

ROBBIE: I don't want you staying here any more, Alice.

ALICE: I have to. I haven't got all my points yet.

ROBBIE: What?

ALICE: Oh don't worry about me, they're looking after me. It's Lyn I'm worried about. Do you think she's getting better? I don't know. That space helmet – do you think, if they implant some sort of tissue in your brain, that you can get someone else's memory mixed up with your own?

ROBBIE: The helmet is not implanting any sort of tissue. The little wires are applying pressure to the neurons. That's all.

ALICE: Do you think we're all made up of the things that happened to us and the things that might have happened as well as things that happened to other people and not being able to distinguish between them is like being in a state of oneness with the universe, like being a baby again, and that it protects you maybe from the reality of your limitations and the knowledge that you're going to die?

ROBBIE: No.

ALICE: I mean what she remembers and what we remember might not be the same thing because it depends on where you were standing at the time, it depends which part of the elephant you've got doesn't it – ear, trunk, no-one has the whole elephant.

ROBBIE: What are you talking about, Alice?

ALICE: She thinks it was me who put their hand in a wasps' nest in Italy.

ROBBIE: It was.

ALICE: It was not! It was her.

ROBBIE: It was you.

ALICE: It was never me. It was Lyn. I remember her screaming. I remember her hand, swollen.

ROBBIE: Alice. You put your hand in the wasps' nest.

ALICE: I didn't.

ROBBIE: You did.

ALICE: How do you know? You weren't even born!

ROBBIE: Yes I was.

ALICE: No, I was five, Lyn was twelve –

ROBBIE: Of course I was *born*.

Beat.

ALICE: Well yes, sorry, alright, of course. But you weren't *there*.

ROBBIE: I remember being told.

Pause.

DYLAN: Do you know, it's weird, but Aunty Lyn doesn't swear so much any more. And she remembers stuff like she's *there*.

ALICE: What's the point of being *there* if she's not *here*? What's the point of that?

Beat.

DYLAN: There's this game, right. It's called Empathyzone. And what you do, you actually get to *be* someone else, it's so cool. You get to wear their clothes and think their thoughts and do their job or whatever, it can be in the old days or now it doesn't matter, and you just, like, experience what they experience. You go inside their head. It's amazing. You can choose a time in history or you just go I'd like to know what it feels like to be rich or whatever, kill someone, like a taboo, that's the number one choice. You go right inside their head and get to feel what it's really like.

ROBBIE: What's the number two choice?

DYLAN: Not saying.

Beat.

ROBBIE: Is it anything to do with –

DYLAN: I'm not telling you Uncle Robbie.

ROBBIE: And you've played this game?

DYLAN: No it's a Fifteen.

ROBBIE looks at his watch.

ROBBIE: Right. *(Gets up to leave and gather his things.)* We have to go. I've got an audition.

ALICE: Another one?

ROBBIE: Yes another one. *(To DYLAN.)* Come on.

DYLAN: I haven't.

ROBBIE: Dylan.

DYLAN: You see. This is the trouble with the older generation. So impatient. It's all me me me. Now now now.

ALICE: Don't you think you should stop this, Robbie?

ROBBIE: Stop what?

ALICE: All this auditioning and acting and rushing about.

ROBBIE: It's called *work*.

ALICE: Yes.

Beat.

ROBBIE: What do you mean?

ALICE: I don't mean because of your… I mean because of your health.

ROBBIE: I do not want to become invisible.

ALICE: Don't you? I've always rather liked the idea of being invisible.

ROBBIE: You don't understand, Alice. You're such a bloody *optimist*. People die. People keep getting ill and dying and when they die they take a little piece of you with them. All the people who know you keep on dying. Or forgetting. And you're left with people who don't know you, who never knew you before you were old, who only know you now, as an old man, so that's what you become. *An old man. (Beat.)* I'm sorry, Alice, I –

ALICE: I'll be fine, Robbie.

ROBBIE: I know, I know.

ALICE: So will you.

DYLAN: Morgue! The missing letter's O. M. O. R. G.

ROBBIE hugs ALICE and ushers DYLAN out with him. She blows kisses after them. ROBBIE and DYLAN continue arguing as they leave.

ROBBIE: That's not how you spell morgue.

DYLAN: How do you spell it then?

ROBBIE: You tell me.

DYLAN: You don't know do you?

ROBBIE: Yes, *I* know how to spell it, I want *you* to tell *me*.

SCENE SIX

HOSPITAL WARD. LYN'S BED.

LYN, MONROE, MIMI.

MONROE eats his way hungrily through LYN'S fruitbowl during the scene.

MONROE: If I was at home we'd be having a party. We always have a party on her birthday. Black tie, magnificent spread, people dancing into the early hours. She sits there on the sofa lapping it all up. Next morning there are usually a few stragglers, we'll go hunting. That's the bit she really likes. The kill and then pheasant for breakfast.

LYN: I like cats.

MONROE: Cats are selfish bastards wouldn't save their own kittens if it meant getting their paws wet. Ffion, on the other hand, would save your life, even if she didn't know you.

LYN: We had a cat. It died.

MIMI makes sympathetic noises. LYN strokes her arm.

MONROE: We're all going to die eventually, Mrs Coulson.

LYN: Well of course we are. *(She yawns.)*

MONROE: I should go.

LYN: Oh I'm always tired.

MONROE: It's the pills.

LYN: No it's not, because I'm not taking them.

MONROE: What do you mean?

LYN: Someone keeps creeping in here, stealing my pills and replacing them with other pills.

Beat.

MONROE: You have to take your pills, Mrs Coulson.

LYN: No, Mr Monroe, not if they're not mine I don't. These are blue, mine are pink.

MONROE: But you have to take a pill. You're being monitored. They can tell if you don't take any pills.

LYN: I'm not being monitored. I told them, I don't want any more of their tests. I want quality of life. They said it's an option. They give you the pink ones and leave you alone.

Beat.

MONROE: So these pink pills, have you got any left at all?

LYN: Only todays.

MONROE: Can I see them?

LYN: They're *pills.* They look exactly the same as yours, only pink. What colour are yours?

MONROE: Blue. Green. Turquoise really.

LYN: Turquoise?

MONROE: Are they in the drawer?

LYN: I'm not telling you, am I? Would you please stop eating all my fruit, Mr Monroe. I'm not a café.

MONROE: *(He stops what he's eating.)* I'm so sorry. My appetite. It's ridiculous.

LYN: Shouldn't you be heading back to your office now?

MONROE: We're in the Ark, Mrs Coulson. Its a hospital.

LYN: Well *I* know that.

MONROE: Do you know what town we're in?

LYN: Yes I know what bloody town we're in. We're in London town.

MONROE: London town.

LYN: Yes.

MONROE: *(He starts eating again.)* What part of London town?

LYN: I don't know. I don't know what part. I've never been
here before, have I? And I'm never coming here again I
can tell you. The food is terrible. And there isn't even a
swimming pool. I like a hotel to have a swimming pool. It's
the least you'd expect for this price, isn't it, Mimi? *(LYNN
and MIMI yawn.)*

MIMI: Are you tired, Lyn?

LYN: Mmm.

MONROE: I should go.

LYN: Yes. Off you go now.

MIMI: I'm tired.

MONROE: Goodbye then, Mrs Coulson.

*MIMI gives LYN's hand a stroke and lays her head on her shoulder.
LYN shuts her eyes.*

*MONROE gets up. He walks around the bed and makes to leave but
hovers, checking that LYN has fallen asleep. He returns to her bedside
and starts going through her drawer. MIMI stirs.*

MIMI: Mmn?

MONROE: It's alright. Just don't – *(MIMI squawks in alarm.
He stops, startled.)* shsh – It's for her own good. It's alright.
Where's she hidden them today? Under the mattress?
No. Under the bed again? *(MIMI murmurs.)* Am I getting
warmer? Am I hot? *(She growls.)* Ssshsh. *(He finds the pills in
a shoe.)* Ah, here we are. Pink pills, you see, useless. These
are the ones she wants. There we are. *(He pockets the pink
pills and replaces them with his blue pills.)* See, everyone's
happy. Okay?

MIMI: Okay.

MONROE: Look.

MIMI: I see.

MONROE: I'm giving her mine. The good pills. And I'm taking hers, the pointless pills. Placebos, good pills, good pills, placebos. *(He downs a couple of her pills with a glass of water.)* Just don't tell anyone, alright?

MIMI: Alright.

MONROE: Good girl. *(She murmurs. He leans right into her face.)* You really are…. something…. *(He hovers close, about to kiss her. She responds by leaning in towards him. She makes a cooing sound and nuzzles him back. At the last moment she licks him. He draws back.)* Jesus. God help me. What am I doing? *(He stands up abruptly and lurches, like a drunk, to one side. Rights himself and walks on. It happens again; he rights himself, walks off.)*

SCENE SEVEN

Hospital ward. Projection: scan of MILLIE'S baby, quite formed now.

CATHY and ROBBIE stand. He's wearing a baseball hat and is dressed, as ever, younger. MILLIE sits.

MILLIE: Did you see the way she looked at me? Prodding around my stomach with her goo stick.

ROBBIE: Did you see the way she looked at *me?*

CATHY: No Robbie we didn't.

MILLIE: Just because I'm *sixteen.* Doesn't mean I'm stupid. I see people looking at me all the time thinking underage, poor thing and stupid cow, they look at me like I'm disgusting, like I'm diseased, like they might catch something.

CATHY: Don't worry about what they think.

MILLIE: I don't. I don't care what people think. I'm having it.

CATHY: I don't think she was thinking that. You're way past that stage, Millie.

MILLIE: Yeah, *I* know that.

CATHY: We all know that.

MILLIE: I know.

ROBBIE: You're fine. You're good.

CATHY: How's your Mum?

MILLIE: Busy.

CATHY: Is she… acclimatised?

MILLIE: I don't know. She's not talking to me. *(Looking at the scan.)* What do you think?

ROBBIE: It's incredible.

MILLIE: Isn't it cool?

CATHY: It's unfeasible.

MILLIE: Paddling about like a little otter. *(Beat.)* How did she look at you?

ROBBIE: Who?

MILLIE: Nursey.

ROBBIE: With suspicion. And a degree of …interest.

MILLIE: Maybe she thought you were the father.

ROBBIE: Hahahaha. Who did you say we were?

MILLIE: Relatives. *(Beat.)* What is it with the hat, uncle Robbie?

ROBBIE: It's a baseball hat.

MILLIE: I've never seen you wear a baseball hat before.

ROBBIE: I've never seen a living, moving creature inside another living moving creature before. *(Beat.)* Is she coming back?

MILLIE: You fancy her.

ROBBIE: I do not fancy her.

MILLIE: No, you're right. She's too old for you.

ROBBIE: She's half my age.

MILLIE: She's never half your age. If she was half your age that would make you a hundred.

CATHY: I don't think we should be here when she gets back. You should have some time – woman to woman – alone with her.

MILLIE: You think I fancy her?

CATHY: Millie.

MILLIE: Please. Don't go.

Beat.

CATHY: Why not?

MILLIE: I'm so scared.

CATHY: What is there to be scared of?

MILLIE: Well. There's miscarriages, there's ectopic pregnancy, there's premature labour, there's the risk of it coming out wrong and last but not least, there's death.

CATHY: I mean now. What is there to be scared of now?

MILLIE: And should we survive all that, baby and me, there's the question of how the hell am I gonna bring it up?

Beat.

ROBBIE: You'll be fine.

MILLIE: How? They don't come with instructions, do they, babies?

ROBBIE: No, it's better than that. They come with buttons.

MILLIE: Buttons?

ROBBIE: Yes. Buttons. You press theirs, they feel something. They press yours, you feel something.

MILLIE: What happens if I *feel* like leaving it on the pavement?

ROBBIE: You won't.

CATHY: And if you do

ROBBIE: It'll pass.

Beat.

MILLIE: What happens. I can't say it. What happens. I can't. What happens. If I don't love it?

ROBBIE: You will.

MILLIE: What happens if it doesn't love me?

ROBBIE: It would be mad.

MILLIE: What happens if it's mad?

ROBBIE: It'll be in good company.

MILLIE: You don't know what you're talking about, Uncle Robbie.

ROBBIE: I was a baby once, you know.

MILLIE: Still are.

ROBBIE: Cathy'll help. Cathy's good with babies.

CATHY: What?

MILLIE: Cathy's never had a baby.

CATHY: I have no idea how to look after a baby.

ROBBIE: Yes you have, I've seen you.

CATHY: You haven't.

ROBBIE: I have. You'd be good at it.

CATHY: How could I possibly look after a child? I can't even look after my own mother, can I?

Beat.

ROBBIE: That's different. It's completely different.

MILLIE: Anyway. I don't need for anyone to look after the baby. Me and Dem will look after the baby. I just don't want you to chuck me or anything.

ROBBIE: We have no intention of chucking you. Have we?

CATHY: No.

MILLIE: Are you crying?

ROBBIE: No I am not crying.

MILLIE: You are, look, there's a tear –

She touches his cheek.

ROBBIE: It's not a tear.

MILLIE: There, look, it's wet.

ROBBIE: I am not crying. Don't. It must be – *(She touches his face again.)* No don't –

MILLIE: It's all sticky.

ROBBIE: Leave it.

CATHY: Millie.

MILLIE: It must be that gel. Ergh look it's got something in it.

ROBBIE: Millie, please

MILLIE: No, Robbie, look –

ROBBIE: Don't

MILLIE: Your face

ROBBIE: Don't touch it.

CATHY: Millie, you mustn't.

MILLIE: There is there's something attached to your face.

She tries to pull a piece of something off his face.

ROBBIE: DON'T TOUCH ME. *(He pulls away and falls off the back of the bed, with a scream of pain.)*

MILLIE: I'm sorry, Robbie, I'm sorry, are you alright? *(Silence.)* Is it your back? I'm so sorry. Oh God, I'll call the nurse. I'm so sorry, I didn't mean to. Can you get up? Don't get up if you can't get up. Oh god, what's happened?

She stands back as he levers himself up by the bed. He stands, looking dishevelled, exhausted and a good twenty years older. In his hand he holds the mask that was his face.

ROBBIE: I told you. Not to touch me.

MILLIE screams her head off.

SCENE EIGHT

HOSPITAL WARD.

MONROE sits, eating. One arm hangs limp at his side. He retrieves two pink pills from a pocket with the other hand. Struggles to get them out of the packet. Eventually he succeeds. He swallows one, then the other. With the same hand he downs a glass of water. There is a banana in his lap. He stares at it. Stares at his limp arm. Pulls it onto his lap with the good arm. He looks at it, willing it to move. It doesn't. He picks up the banana with his good hand and tries to manoeuvre the other one across to peel it. It's no good. He studies the paralysed hand. Tries getting the fingers to move. Cheats them into action by manoeuvring the tendons with his other hand. He lowers his head to the banana but can't take the top off. Instead he sinks his teeth angrily into his hand. But of course feels no pain. He yells in frustration.

SCENE NINE

LYN'S ROOM.

MILLIE, LYN, DYLAN, CATHY, ALICE, all in funereal black.

MILLIE'S baby's in it's cot. ALICE, in a wheelchair. One of her hands is bandaged and she has a tube coming out of her nose. LYN is fussing about, moving chairs.

 Silence.

DYLAN: In the in the in the

CATHY: Crematorium.

DYLAN: Yeah. What was the curtain for?

CATHY: I don't know. It's just a tradition.

DYLAN: But who was like, operating it?

CATHY: It's automatic.

DYLAN: Did the coffin have speakers in?

CATHY: No.

DYLAN: So where was the music coming from?

CATHY: I don't know Dylan.

 Beat.

DYLAN: When it went through. The curtain. Where did it go?

CATHY: Underneath the thing.

ALICE: On a journey.

DYLAN: What thing?

CATHY: Some sort of chamber.

DYLAN: Is that where the actual body is?

CATHY: No.

DYLAN: Where is it?

CATHY: It's not.

DYLAN: What then?

ALICE: He'll be half way to heaven by now.

DYLAN: What then?

CATHY: Cremated.

DYLAN: Burnt, you mean?

CATHY nods. DYLAN bursts into tears. She comforts him.

LYN: I'm so glad you could all come. It's very cramped here I'm afraid, I don't know how we're going to dance. There aren't even enough chairs. What are we going to do, Mimi?

MIMI makes sympathetic noises.

LYN: Isn't she wonderful? We need another chair Alice. Why don't you sit on the bed?

CATHY: Mum.

ALICE: I can't.

LYN: Don't be silly, no-one minds.

CATHY: It's a wheelchair, Mum. Her leg.

LYN takes a good look at ALICE.

LYN: Why's she got her hand bandaged then? Why have you got that thing coming out of your nose?

ALICE: Tests.

LYN: What for?

ALICE: Obesity.

LYN: You're not *obese.*

ALICE: No but other people are.

LYN: Well *(To CATHY.)* you can stand up. Let Mimi have your chair, go on, darling, she's been on her feet all day, haven't you? *(She ushers MIMI towards CATHY's chair.)*

MIMI: I'm fine.

CATHY: She's fine.

LYN: Robbie'll get one. Where is Robbie? Has he gone to get one? Robbie!

The baby gurgles happily. CATHY gets up and sits on the edge of LYN's bed. LYN urges MIMI to take CATHY's seat. She does.

CATHY: Mum.

ALICE: Don't.

LYN: And they said they'd provide the music. A bit of swing they said but there's no sign of any equipment. We'll just have to sing ourselves, won't we? *(She starts to hum. MIMI mimics her.)* Oh they're such a bunch of miseryguts my family. Look at you all huddled round like penguins in a storm. I'm trying to make an effort and you're all – have I died? Is that why you're all ignoring me? Well if this is death it's not half as bad as I thought although it's hot enough to grow tomatoes in here. How did I die I wonder?

She pinches CATHY. CATHY jumps.

CATHY: Ow.

LYN: Sorry.

Silence.

MILLIE: About a month ago Dylan, me and Robbie were having an arm wrestle. You know what he's like, he let us win and I said I like the way you always let us win and he said would you still like me if I didn't? And I said we love you as you are Uncle Robbie and he said you don't know me as I am and I said what're you going on about? And then he said would you still love me if I was old and I said of course I would, why? And he said he wasn't sure. Wasn't sure if we loved him or wasn't sure why he was asking? I didn't know. I still don't know. *(Silence.)* Were we not enough?

ALICE: Oh Millie.

DYLAN: I mean did they shoot him or what?

CATHY: No Dylan they didn't shoot him.

DYLAN: Or what. I said or what.

ALICE: They let him go. Gently.

DYLAN: *How?*

CATHY: They gave him a pill.

ALICE: A little pill.

DYLAN: What kind of pill?

ALICE: Like a sleeping pill.

DYLAN: They killed him.

CATHY: Yes.

ALICE: No. No, he asked for it.

DYLAN: Why?

ALICE: He was eighty five, you know.

MILLIE: I know.

DYLAN: So what?

CATHY: They stopped his treatment.

DYLAN: What treatment?

ALICE: He had internal trouble. And once they found out his real age they took away his pills.

DYLAN: Why?

CATHY: No longer cost effective.

ALICE: The thing is. Once you reach a certain age. He didn't want to become. The thing is, he had a good life. He loved his job and he just wanted to carry on but if you've had a good life – he won't have suffered you know, at the end. He's just moving on to another better place. It's alright. Just like it's alright to rest when you've finished work. Or lie down if you're sleepy –

DYLAN: Or kill people if you hate them.

ALICE: yes.

CATHY: No.

ALICE: No. What did he say?

MILLIE: What about us? What about me? What about George?

The baby gurgles happily.

LYN: I know what it is. It's Peter. You don't have to go all hush hush. I know exactly what happened because Cathy told me. It's not a shock. We've all known about him being ill since the coughing incident.

CATHY: Robbie, Mum. It's Robbie who's died.

MONROE comes running on. He stops suddenly at the sight of them.

MONROE: Mrs Coulson, have you seen – oh ladies. Ladies. I'm so sorry.

LYN: Mr Monroe.

MONROE: I didn't realise.

LYN: What is it?

MONROE: They're everywhere.

LYN: Who?

MONROE: Haven't you seen them? Look! The whole place is overrun. There must be a special aviary nearby. But you'd think someone would have noticed, wouldn't you? Look, look, there's another one!

CATHY: I'm sorry, but we're in the middle of –

MONROE: No, it's my fault, I didn't realise you were having a

CATHY: Funeral.

MONROE: I just wanted – oh look, there's one behind the curtain! Will you look at those colours. I never realised they were so bright. I'm sorry, please excuse me.

He follows the imaginary bird off. Silence.

LYN: Schizophrenic. Thinks he works for the government. Keeps stealing my pills. *(Beat.)* I'm shaking. Why am I shaking?

CATHY: You've had a shock.

LYN: I feel… abandoned. Oh, Mimi. I feel completely

CATHY makes to comfort her but LYN cuddles up to MIMI instead.

MIMI: Abandoned.

LYN: Again.

MIMI: Not again.

LYN: Like when I was a little girl.

MIMI: When you were a little girl.

LYN: She left me all alone and I had to fend for myself

MIMI: Like an orphan.

LYN: Yes, like an orphan.

MIMI: Poor orphan.

LYN: And again that time with Peter.

MIMI: Peter. Abandoned you.

LYN: Abandoned me.

MIMI: Again.

LYN: Then there was the French woman.

MIMI: From France.

LYN: People are always leaving me.

MIMI: Always.

LYN: It's hard.

MIMI: It's very hard.

LYN: Don't cry.

MIMI: No, don't cry.

LYN: It's going to be alright.

MIMI: Alright. It's alright.

LYN: That's better. Mummy loves you. There there.

CATHY: NO YOU DON'T, YOU DON'T KNOW WHAT YOU'RE TALKING ABOUT. WHAT ARE YOU TALKING ABOUT?!

ALICE: Cathy, Cathy, Cathy

CATHY: YOU DON'T LOVE HER AND SHE COULDN'T GIVE A FUCK ABOUT YOU. SHE'S A *MACHINE*.

MIMI starts squawking in distress.

LYN: Why are you shouting?

CATHY: Robbie, YOUR BROTHER, IS *DEAD*. He's dead, Mum. Dad died eight years ago. This is Robbie we're talking about. Not Dad.

ALICE: Cathy. I don't think we should –

CATHY: *SHE'S MY MOTHER.*

ALICE: She's my sister but –

CATHY: She's my mother and your sister how can that be interfering? Somebody's died and it's your *brother* and she doesn't understand. *She doesn't understand.*

ALICE: I don't understand. *(ALICE tries to protect MIMI from LYN.)* No, don't, CATHY, don't.

CATHY: Come here.

ALICE: Leave it, she needs her robot, she loves it.

CATHY: IT'S A *MACHINE*. YOU CANNOT LOVE A MACHINE. IT HAS NOTHING TO DO WITH LOVE. Come here you fucking *robot*.

ALICE: I don't think you should touch

CATHY grabs MIMI. MIMI cries out in distress.

LYN: Leave her alone.

CATHY: Where are your batteries?

CATHY hits out at her.

MIMI: No. No. No. Not. No.

MIMI backs away. CATHY circles her. MIMI growls.

CATHY: Dylan? Batteries.

LYN: Leave my friend alone.

DYLAN: She'll have a chip in the back somewhere. But I think you should –

CATHY: Keep still, WITCH!

MIMI: *(MIMI squeals and beeps.)* Keep which. Keep. Is that better? Still. ....eurgh

CATHY: *Shuttup.* Keep still. There. *(CATHY has her now. Pulls out a connection in her back.)*

LYN: No! *(MIMI flails about and lets out a series of electronic beeps.)* Mimi come back. Don't go. Come back! *(MIMI lets out a final whirring screech and collapses.)* She's dead.

CATHY: She was never alive.

DYLAN: I don't think you should have done that, Aunty Cath.

LYN: What have you done you cow? She was my friend.

CATHY: No. She wasn't.

LYN: She was my only friend.

CATHY: No.

LYN: She loved me, she understood me

CATHY: No no no , you don't need to be understood. You need to understand. You need to *understand.* It's not your fault I haven't had children I never said it was. It's not my fault you haven't got a grandchild. It's not your fault and it's not my fault. We're not the same person and I can't be what you want me to be because I'm *real.* I'm not a *mirror,* that's all she is, and I don't care what you call me as long as you know the difference. Do you understand?

LYN: I have got a grandchild.

CATHY: Do you understand *me?*

LYN: I hate you.

Beat.

CATHY: Who?

LYN: *You you.*

CATHY: Who am I?

LYN: Don't be stupid. You're my bloody daughter Catherine and I have got a grandchild.

Beat.

111

CATHY: Right.

LYN: I hate you.

CATHY: I hate you too Mum.

Silence. After a while CATHY holds out her hand to LYN. LYN takes it warmly.

LYN: Where on earth have you been? We've been looking for you everywhere. I thought you'd gone to Brazil and left me holding the thing. Do you know, when you were born, you had the most beautiful head I've ever seen. Like a like a like a fabulous egg.

Silence. MILLIE takes George out of his basket.

MILLIE: Would anyone like to look after him a minute?

ALICE: Ooh yes please.

ALICE holds out her hands.

DYLAN: Can I have a go?

CATHY: I will.

In the confusion MILLIE trips over ALICE's foot; the baby goes flying. He is suspended in mid air both on the screen and off. The image of the baby is projected as it falls, slowly, becoming a turtle, itself again, an old man, a turtle, itself again. DYLAN rushes to catch the baby as ALICE gets up. He knocks her back down again. But not before her leg, in perfect shape and with high heeled shoe, is revealed.

CATHY steps forward; a moment later and the baby falls into her arms.

ALICE: I'm sorry, I'm so sorry. It's my leg. I can't feel a thing.

DYLAN: Are you alright? *(He struggles to help her back into her chair.)*

ALICE: I'm fine.

MILLIE: Is he alright?

CATHY: He's beautiful.

DYLAN: Your leg, Nan.

ALICE: Isn't it good?

DYLAN: It's amazing. The shoes and everything.

ALICE: They came with it. *(She flexes her leg.)* I chose the dancer's leg.

DYLAN: So why are you still in the wheelchair?

ALICE: Oh I can't walk on it. It's aesthetic.

CATHY: Prosthetic.

ALICE: No, aesthetic. While they see if the new cells take.

The baby gurgles.

DYLAN: Is he real? He looks like a doll.

CATHY: I'll look after him, Millie. I'll help you look after him.

MILLIE: I didn't mean for ever. I just meant for, like, a minute.

Beat.

CATHY: Mum. Do you want to? *(She proffers the baby.)*

LYN: Oh yes please! I'll hold it.

CATHY hands the baby to LYN. LYN cuddles him.

LYN: I love turtles.

Beat.

CATHY: That's good.

THE END